Sumerians

Legacy of the Ancient Mesopotamian Empire

(A Comprehensive Guide to Sumerian Mythology Including Myths)

Michael Miller

Published By **Darby Connor**

Michael Miller

All Rights Reserved

Sumerians: Legacy of the Ancient Mesopotamian Empire (A Comprehensive Guide to Sumerian Mythology Including Myths)

ISBN 978-1-77485-494-5

No part of this guidebook shall be reproduced in any form without permission in writing from the publisher except in the case of brief quotations embodied in critical articles or reviews.

Legal & Disclaimer

The information contained in this ebook is not designed to replace or take the place of any form of medicine or professional medical advice. The information in this ebook has been provided for educational & entertainment purposes only.

The information contained in this book has been compiled from sources deemed reliable, and it is accurate to the best of the Author's knowledge; however, the Author cannot guarantee its accuracy and validity and cannot be held liable for any errors or omissions. Changes are periodically made to this book. You must consult your doctor or get professional medical advice before using any of the suggested remedies, techniques, or information in this book.

Upon using the information contained in this book, you agree to hold harmless the

Author from and against any damages, costs, and expenses, including any legal fees potentially resulting from the application of any of the information provided by this guide. This disclaimer applies to any damages or injury caused by the use and application, whether directly or indirectly, of any advice or information presented, whether for breach of contract, tort, negligence, personal injury, criminal intent, or under any other cause of action.

You agree to accept all risks of using the information presented inside this book. You need to consult a professional medical practitioner in order to ensure you are both able and healthy enough to participate in this program.

Table of Contents

Chapter 1 Sumer's History History Of Sumer 1

Chapter 2: Importance Of Religion In Sumerian Civilization 23

Chapter 3: Lighter Tales Of Sumerian Gods And Heroes 55

Chapter 4: Akkadian Empire And Mythology 61

Chapter 5: Twenty Vital Facts Concerning Sumerian History And Mythology 69

Chapter 6: Contributions 129

Chapter 7: Sumerian Literature 137

Chapter 8: The Sumerian Motivation And System Of Values 152

Chapter 9: The Importance Of Sumerian Heroes And Rulers ...156

Chapter 10: Secret Life Of Sumer .177

Conclusion 180

Chapter 1 Sumer's History History of Sumer

Mesopotamia is among areas that is the most productive on Earth. It is a plain that lies between two rivers which are that is the Euphrates River and the Tigris River It is strategically situated in a place that is located in Asia yet is close to both Africa and Africa in Europe. It is possible that this is the reason this region hasn't only provided the foundation for many of the most significant civilizations throughout history however, it has also been constantly battled by groups of all kinds, including those of the Egyptians, Romans, and Ottoman Turks. Mesopotamia was a country worth acquiring and many conquerors, like Alexander the Great were aware of the importance of it.

The majority of Mesopotamia is currently located in the country of Iraq However, portions of it are located in Turkey, Syria, and the rest of the nations. It is not even including the countries directly surrounding Mesopotamia which were subjected to the cultural and political influences of this significant region. It is believed that the Greeks and Macedonians were only a few of the numerous people who understood the importance of the region. The Seleucids who took power after the death Alexander established their capital city in Seleucia situated on Tigris within Mesopotamia. They were aware that not only the fertile plain that surrounded the city thriving however, it also provided an ideal watchtower to observe and observe the Persians, Bactrians, and other people who wanted to fight for their freedom.

The chapter that follows we'll look at the development of Mesopotamia with a focus specifically on that of the Sumerian period. Since the Sumerian gods were also featured as gods in other pantheons and civilisations in the region, we'll review other empires that came and went following that of Sumerian or Akkadian states. One of the most important points to be out from the way immediately is to note that the majority of historians believe Mesopotamia to be the origin of the civilizations. The first proof of the existence of writing or living (to the present day) is not in Egypt or even Europe and not in Europe, rather in Mesopotamia.

The theory is that Mesopotamia was continuously inhabited for at most 12,000 years. Its climate, suitability to cultivate, as well as its the abundant water supply, both clean and fresh water were ideal to start an ancient civilization. As you'll see the first cities of the region flourished around 6000 years long ago.

A Brief Overview of Mesopotamian History

Mesopotamia was a region of rival city-states in the time from 4000 BC until around 3000 BC. The cities would later be united under King Sargon who was a member of the Akkadian Empire. They would remain together under the rule of both the Assyrians along with the Babylonians. The region was noted for the constant battles that did not stop major advances in agriculture or the high civilization from forming. The size of the buildings was immense in Mesopotamia which included the Ziggurats, which were constructed to enable interaction to gods. Sumerian gods.

People from Mesopotamia were not just notable for their agricultural and religion but also for their achievements in the fields of math and science. Certain practices that were created during this time period are still used today. These advances in mathematics included the sixty-second minute sixty minute hour as well as the circle that was made up from three hundred sixty degrees. One of the most important uses of these mathematical techniques was astronomy.

The Babylonians For instance, they separated the calendar into 12 seasons. Each of the twelve periods was given an inscription that referred to the most famous night sky constellation which is essentially a zodiac system that is still in use in a few religions and cultures in the present. The seven-day weekend is something which can also be attributed to the gods of Babylonians. The most significant development of those of Mesopotamia however, is thought to be the method of writing.

The system started out as pictographs that were similar to hieroglyphics used by ancient Egypt. Ancient Egyptians. The system would later evolve into what we recognize today as writing. This writing system started to emerge around 3200 BC. It is now referred to as cuneiform. It was so adaptable that it became the basis for over twelve languages, including Babylonian, Hittite, Persian and Elamite. Hammurabi's Code is the oldest law code of its kind was written in cuneiform script that people from Mesopotamia came up with.

Mesopotamia's wealth, both material as well as intellectual, could eventually be the reason for its demise. Cities such as Babylon were too attractive for foreigners to not be regarded as targets for invasion. From the time of the conquest of Babylon by the Persians in 539 BC, Mesopotamia would find itself under the control of foreigners. Mesopotamia would be placed in the category of nations that were second rate under the control of other nations. The city would vanish into the sandsof time, but its history of science, language and mathematics would endure until the present day.

The Sumerians

Some believe individuals that the change from hunter-gathering communities and large agriculture societies was made during Mesopotamia in the period between 10,000 BC between 4000 and 10,000 BC. In the Sumerian civilisation, you have the first evidence that is documented of the wheel and astronomy, the language along with the division of the time. The first cities that were truly built are also being developed in Sumer the region of Southern Mesopotamia.

The first citied was part of The Ubaid Culture of Sumer, which was in existence from around 6000 BC until around 4000 BC. Migration waves swept from the coast regions to the West and, in the present-day Syria as well as across Syria, and into the Mesopotamian plains. The Sumerian culture was developed by the interplay of these cities. These cities in Sumer comprised Kish, Ur, Eridu, Nippur, Uruk, and Babylon. Since there was a surplus of food in these cities, the majority of the population was able engage in other activities that allowed for the development of Mesopotamia which were previously described.

The cities of Sumer created rivalries with each other and attracted foreigners. The first cities that were walled were built at places like Uruk. In the end, all largest cities within Sumer were walled. About the year 2500 BC, Enshakushanna, king of Uruk was able to conquer the majority of the cities-states from Sumer in the name of "Lord of Sumer." His reign was not long since a rival king was set to besiege Uruk and the city-states of the past which were dependent on Uruk. In this period, Sumerian kings conquered the adjacent kingdom of Mari and even won the battle in the East in The Elamite capital city Susa.

Around one hundred years after, a man from Kish was elevated from the position of cupbearer and conquered the city in Kish in addition to Uruk. This was Sargon the creator of Akkad. The time period of Sumerian time was one of integration. This was crucial in Sumerian history because city states were distinct as virtual nations. Sargon permitted Sumer along with Akkad to form an identity as a united Mesopotamian nation.

The Akkadians

Sargon's ambitions were not over when he had unification of his cities in Sumer in the southern part of Mesopotamia. Sargon continued to conquer the entire city and other cities in the fertile plain of Mesopotamia. He established an empire. in actual fact, the empire that was Sargon was believed by a lot of historians to be the first empire in history. This was an empire since Sargon was the ruler of people who were multilingual and had their own distinct administrations.

At the time of his reign that he was in charge, the original language of Sumerians was replaced by a script of Semitic origin. Sumerians was replaced by the script that was Semitic Origins (i.e. that of to the Eastern Mediterranean to the West of Sumer). His state was dubbed The Akkadian Empire and it would remain with the descendants of Sargon for more than two hundred years. In this period an additional state east of Sumer named Susa was to rise to prominence. The Susans were strong enough and advanced enough to compete with the Akkadians to gain influence within the region.

This period also witnessed the growth of the Gutian people as a potential threat towards the Akkadians. The Gutians were able to attack the Akkadians causing the gradual decline of the Akkadian Empire. They would then burn Akkad which was the capital for The Akkadians to the level of the earth. The exact location of Akkad is still a mystery however archaeologists and historians have utilized evidence from the time and later to establish an idea of the location the city could be. A lot of people believe it's close in the vicinity of Baghdad that is the capital city of the current Iraqi nation. Iraq.

The Akkadians were to be replaced politically within the area by the Neo-Sumerian Empire, which is sometimes referred to in the Third Dynasty of Ur. This time period that was part of the Neo-Sumerian Empire lasted from around 2100 BC until around 2000 BC. The period ended due to the deprecation of the Amorites which was an Arabian tribe from the south that was becoming more prominent. The Amorites were to adopt the beliefs and practices of the Neo-Sumerians and establish their capital in
Babylon. Babylon would later turn into

one of the well-known cities in the world.

Another important point to consider regarding one of the most important aspects to consider about Akkadian as well as the Neo-Sumerian the period of time is that historians call the widespread bilingualism of that period. At the time, though Akkadian was in a few ways substituting Sumerian in terms of administrative functions, the general population was mostly bilingual, speaking the two languages, Akkadian as well as Sumerian. It wasn't till when it was the Amorite time that Akkadian completely took over Sumerian as an administrative as well as a known language of Mesopotamia.

Evidence of the significance of Akkadian can be found by the name of city kings, such as Assur as well as Eshnunna. Today, the centre of religious activities was the Nippur. Nippur. The city of Nippur Enlil was the main god. Enlil would be the ultimate divinity in Sumer until the advent from Babylon during the period of 18 century BC. It was Amor, the Amorites as well as one of their King's, Hammurabi, who would be the ones responsible for the development of Babylon as a major city.

There are the Amorites and Amurru

There's been a lot of confusion and misinformation about the Amorites. The racist theorists of late 19th-early 20th century believed it was because the Amorites were Aryans, who differed from other indigenous peoples in the region. They arrived at this conclusion based on the narrative that has been handed throughout the centuries specifically they claimed that Amorites are tall. Many even believed that the kings David or Jesus had been "Aryan" Amorites, even the fact that there is no evidence to support this claim. The present day, historians are aware they believe that Amorites were clearly Semitic group that may be similar to the Canaanites who lived throughout the Southern Levant before the arrival of the Jews from Egypt.

Amurru was the title that was used to a particular group of people (who we today recognize in the form of Amorites) as well as for the god they worshipped. The god they worshipped was also known as Martu and his significant city was known as Ninab. As with other cities in that region, exact place of this city is not understood by archaeologists and historians. Amurru Martu and Martu are recorded in writings from both Akkadian and Sumerian languages.

Amurru was believed to be goddess for Amurru was believed to be the god of Amorite people. The Amorites were originally people of the tribal, uncivilized who lived at the edge of Akkadian as well as the Neo-Sumerian empires. They were pastoralists and were often referred to as the people from the mountains or the steppe. Because of this, Amurru (the God of the gods) was also known as the lord of the mountain or the lord of the steppe. In the role of lord of the mountain, Amurru was called Bel Sade which translates to the same thing. This has caused confusing scholars because one of the gods of Abraham was also known as Bel Sade (lord of the mountain). There was a belief that this god evolved into the famous God of Baal, the god of Bible, Baal.

While not much focus has been paid to the gods of the region the moment it is a great point to start with a discussion about one. While Amurru technically wasn't a god with rigid Sumerian origins, due to the fact that the Amorites defeated Mesopotamia and created the cities of Babylon their capital city, Amurru was able to become an idol that was worshipped by the Sumerian population of Mesopotamia were worshipped by, and is included as one of the Sumerian gods of the present (of which it is said to be more than 3000). Amurru is usually described as being a shepherd, or god of the storm. Its existence Amurru indicates the duality of Gods throughout Sumerian cultural and historical context. It was a god of the region that was later incorporated into the many gods revered by people from Mesopotamia. The gods played two roles: divinities from specific locations or peoples they first worshipped, as well as gods of larger nationalities and empires. This duality that is amazing within Mesopotamians. Mesopotamians is also evident to some extent in the Greeks in their civic love for the gods of this or that.

The Assyrians

The Assyrians are among the few people mentioned in this book that remain in existence to the current. The Assyrians are considered to be an indigenous group from their region of the Middle East. They are also referred to in the form of Syriacs, Chaldeans, and Arameans. They reside mainly within Northern Iraq, Turkey, and Eastern Syria, regions which are considered to be their home and comprised one of the main regions within the Assyrian Empire. The majority of Assyrians are Christian however, earlier, the Assyrians may have worshipped gods like those of the Mesopotamian neighbors.

It is believed that the Assyrian Empire along with its inhabitants have their name derived from Assur, the capital city. Assur. It was a major city particularly during the Akkadian period as well as the centuries that followed it. Kists of Assyrian Kingships from the early time are still around. A majority of them been local potentates, ruling as vassals to one of the Akkadian or Neo-Sumerian King. There are Assyrian cities Assur and Nineveh are documented from as early as 2500 BC even though they were not city-states at the time.

It is believed that the Assyrian period is split into sections based on period of empire and independence of the Assyrians. The first statehood period was called The Early Assyrian Period, although the initial phase of empires was called the Old Assyrian Empire. At the time it was the Assyrian state controlled the entire Mesopotamian area, which the indigenous people of the region considered to be all four regions of the earth. The states were bordered by Zagros Mountains to the East as well as to the West, Caucasus Mountains in the North as well as The Arabian Desert in the South along with the Mediterranean Sea to the West.

The capital of the original State was Assur however, later capitals included Shubat Enlil and Nineveh. The first ruler in the Old Assyrian Empire was Puzur-Ashur I. He was followed by numerous great rulers for a time exceeding 600 years. The fact that the Sumerians were bilingual Sumerians in the previous period is already being examined. The time of the Assyrian Empire, the Assyrians were a dialect of the

Akkadian language. Inscriptions written by them were in a script called Old Assyrian.

The Assyrians were adherents to their polytheistic Mesopotamian religion. The central figure of the Assyrian pantheon was their god of nationality, Assur (or Ashur) as well as Amurru to the Amorites also shared the same name with the Amorites. It's a bizarre coincidence that this shared name can be seen at the site of Athens in which Athena was revered. Other gods of the Assyrian pantheon were Adad, Ninurta, Ninlil, Nergal, Sin, and Ishtar (or Inanna).

It is believed that the Old Assyrian Empire may have been the first major phase in the Assyrian state however it wasn't solely the case. Also, there was The Middle Assyrian Empire, which ran from 1400 BC up to around 900 BC as well as it was followed by the Neo-Assyrian Empire, which occurred between the 900th year BC until about 600 BC.

Babylonians Babylonians

In the Assyrian period, Babylon was an important city, which gradually increased in importance and became one of the biggest cities in the region. Much like the Assyrians there were many periods when Babylon was a state. Babylonian state was an influential regional force, and even as an empire. The situation gets a bit confusing during the time period from 2000 BC until 1300 BC since there were several important states that competed for power, specifically that of the Old Assyrian Empire and the First Babylonian Dynasty.

It is believed that the First Babylonian Dynasty was important due to the fact that the ruler of it was the most well-known in the history of the world Hammurabi. As we have already said, Hammurabi was an Amorite who was famous due to the laws he codified that was his last act. The Amorites came out of in the Levantine coastline to become the rulers in Mesopotamia and the surrounding regions previously called Sumer as well as Akkad. It was the First Babylonian Dynasty lasted from around 1900 BC up to around 1600 BC. The first dynasty started to fall rapidly after Hammurabi's death. It broke up into several states, and the northern region was destroyed. The Babylon city Babylon was itself sacked by the Hittites, an important population whose territory was mostly in Turkey. The Hittites also were known for their victory over the Egyptians in the battle. The Egyptians identified them as the Hyksos. they were the main reason for closing their time in the Middle Period of Egyptian history and eventually led to the Egyptian golden age during the New Period. When exactly the date was the first sack to be thrown into Babylon isn't known however, it is dating between 1499 BC to 1736 BC.

Because Babylon was situated so centrally it was an integral part of several other states and empires in the region. The time of destabilization is followed by three major periods that were centered around Babylon. They were three important periods: the Kassite Period, the Iron Age Period as well as the Neo-Babylonian Empire. This period is called the Chaldean Period, and it was a time of 620 BC until around 539 BC. This time period is famous due to its frequent mention throughout the Old Testament of the Bible. In the Bible, the Chaldean also known as the Neo-Babylonian Empire is the name given to the state of King Nebuchadnezzar. The Bible declares him" the one who destroyed the nations" It was during this time period that Daniel was taken to the lion's cave according to The Holy Book.

The Phoenicians

The Phoenicians were one of the most powerful peoples of the region even though they technically were not in Mesopotamia. The cities along their coasts are predominantly in the present-day region of Lebanon which was known from antiquity for its scented cedarwood. The city-state model was important in the early times and Phoenicia was a country of city-states, more so than of the national empire.

While the Phoenicians might seem to be a minor part of the narrative of Mesopotamia and the Sumerians They were crucial in transferring a lot the essence of Sumerian lifestyle and customs to people who were not from in the Near East, namely the Greeks. We've already discovered the fact that one of the goddesses from the Greek pantheon was from Near Eastern origin. It was Aphrodite which is a descendent of Ashtoreth, the Phoenician goddess, Ashtoreth. Ashtoreth, herself, is descended by Ashtoreth, the Sumerian goddess Inanna or Ishtar.

Although Aphrodite of the Greeks was denuded of all the foreign accouterments that characterized Inanna/Ishtar/Ashtoreth, she still stands out as a white elephant among the Olympians. The sensual nature of her, the magnetism and complete independence from men all indicate that she was both of pre-Greek and non-Greek origin. Aphrodite is not the only goddess who snoozes and spits over her husband Hephaestus However, she also is able to create a strong character that is stronger than many other Greek gods due to her worship. Her worship remains non-Greek in its nature. In fact, goddesses such as Athena and Aphrodite are a symbol of the beliefs of the Sumerians maybe more so than others Greek gods. While historians today refer to with the invaders who landed in Greece during the 2nd millennium and later, as patriarchal people obsessed by the gods of the sky, it's important to note that not all the gods that were introduced in this time were male.

While not all of the Gods from the Phoenicians were able to make their way to the Greeks but they did have Phoenician influence was evident. In fact, the Greek alphabet was influenced to some degree by Phoenician influences. Phoenician alphabet. Phoenician was an Semitic language that was closely related with other languages of the Semitic language family. The Phoenicians had their own god-like pantheon, but they remained in the general Mesopotamian style of worshipping a broad range of gods, most of them were from outside their own nation. Phoenicia was significant historically due to the fact that its cities such as Tyre or Biblos were crucial in the founding of cities such as Carthage which later was one of the biggest empires of the Mediterranean prior to the advent of Rome.

The Persians

Even though the Phoenicians were influential in the history of the world, it would be the Persians who would bring about this Babylonian autonomy in that

Neo-Babylonian (or Chaldean period. The Bible describes the coming of the Persians and their impact on the course of history in the region for ever. After the arrival of the Persians, Mesopotamia would no anymore be the mainstay of the empire but instead an marketplace within bigger and more significant states.

The Persians were the most powerful empire that has ever existed to this date. They controlled the entire region across the deserts in the East up to the mountainous regions of Europe towards the West. They also ruled a large portion in Northern Africa, namely Egypt that was regarded as being among the longest-lasting and richest states in history. It was believed that the Persians were a god-like people with their own deities and after their arrival at the time of the Mesopotamian gods witnessed that they were nearing their decline. The Persian Empire was to be then followed by the Empire of Alexander that would then be eventually followed by Seleucid Empire. The Seleucids were then later followed by the Parthians, who later on would become followed by Sassanians. The Sassanians were the final important country in the area prior the advent of Islam however, by the time they arrived the fire that was the Mesopotamian gods was already nearly been extinguished.

Chapter 2: Importance Of Religion In Sumerian Civilization

The system of religion for the people living in this region Sumer region was extremely complicated with hundreds of gods and gods. Though it began with the worship of nature, with time Sumerian gods were transformed into human-like, and the gods as human beings were believed to hold power over the forces of nature.

Similar to the gods of earlier civilizations Their gods included all the human treaties that they cherished and resented the world, fought and negotiated as well as drank and ate they were married and divorced. Each god was given a status within the hierarchy, abided by specific rules , and ensuring that the universe functioned in a proper manner throughout the day. These rules were referred to as "me."

It's not difficult to determine from where Sumerian theologians got their ideas. Since all things on earth were governed and controlled by humans and their petty egos, it is only natural to suppose that the whole universe and the realm of gods worked exactly the same way. According to the same logic, gods should be eternal. In the absence of that, the universe will be in a state of chaos when they die.

The extremely diverse pantheon of the ancient Sumer included a variety of goddesses and gods most of them were connected to one another through familial ties or service. The four main gods Sumerians identified were An, Enki, Enlil and Ninhursag. They are the ones who created all things including Enlil being the King of the heavens and earth and all gods. Ninhursag is the mother of all creatures.

The Sumerian Pantheon was envisioned much because of its resemblance to human society. The gods of the Sumerian Pantheon were not all of equal importance and not all were equally significant. It is easy to understand why the people from Sumer believed in the god of the sun for instance, in more respect than the God of mold and bricks. The supreme god was chosen and acknowledged in all Gods much like the King was acknowledged by his people.

When it comes to creation, Sumerians had a rather straightforward explanation. However, unlike earlier peoples, didn't have a detailed account of how the world was created. The gods of heaven could create without words. They gave orders, and then things and creatures emerged. Also, if humans could do many things with his words alone, swiftly bending subjects to his wishes, what could it be for supreme God-like creatures?

The idea of "me," the information that is mainly contained in the story in the myth of "Inanna or Enki," also serves to explain the nature of the universe which are akin to humans. As members of the human race gods must abide to certain rules and carry out specific obligations. That is how you can ensure the system running smoothly and keep the chaos at bay.

The worship of their gods was the primary reason for the people from Sumer. But, they believed that the gods of heaven had more important business (like controlling the universe and creating the future) than listening to the common people express their worries and accepting their sacrifices. In consequence, an entire system made up of gods who were personal to them was established.

They were "smaller" gods are believed to dwell in the temples of cities and served as intermediaries between the masses and gods. In the Sumerian epic "The The Creation," the people were created so that they could worship gods and let them quit doing good work. Sumerian gods are charming brutal, uncompromising, and extremely demanding.

This resulted in the creation of temples and religion an ideal foundation for formation of larger communities. As the people had no influence over the decisions of gods and decisions, the most they could expect was that their prayers will be more heard when they united in their requests.

From the various writings of the past from the past, we can see that Sumerian gods were in favor of the truth and justice, but their motivations were elusive to comprehend for the average man. They were far from home and on the mountain from which sunrise was the only thing that could be seen, their beliefs were distant as well as mystical, and difficult to comprehend.

The notion of immortality for gods was frequently questioned in the old Sumerian writings. By default, all deities were immortal. Being anthropomorphic however they were required to eat and drink , and were susceptible to various illnesses that could lead them to the edge of death. They participated in battles, suffered injuries and, in some cases, even killed. This is prevalent in the later religions too, such as that of Egyptian, Greek, and Roman. These attempts at explaining this paradox were frequently made, but failed in reconciling the unconvincing notion that immortal creatures are destined to death.

It is apparent to us that Sumerian civilization was heavily based on the religion of. Actually, everything they did was driven by the desire to satisfy the gods who's mood was extremely inconsistent.

It is not a detriment to their achievements, however but it does suggest that understanding Sumerian society is difficult without knowing their motivations. So, we'll name some of the more significant gods, and then discuss the top important myths that were component of Sumerian society.

Gods

An Anu, also known as ("heavens") Was at first the god of supreme power in The Sumerian Pantheon. He was the god who ruled gods and men and gods, adjusting their positions at the whim of. He is often credited with the creation of everything whether by himself or with the aid from Enki or Enlil.

While the earliest Sumerian writings do not make any reference to the story of An's birth However, later writings refer to An as the son of both Anshar and Kishar the gods of the primordial world which are mentioned only by name in the "Babylon Creation Story."

An is often referred to by the name of one of the "father of gods" since numerous Sumerian gods are believed to have been his sons. Based on the sources of literature We can discover names such as Enki, Nanna, Enlil, Inanna, Nanaya and numerous others.

There were numerous temples scattered throughout Mesopotamia that were dedicated to An. In the third millennium, it is believed that he is worshiped alongside goddess Inana. The place where he was worshiped was Erech, the city Erech in the region of Erech, which seems to have played a important role in the early stages of Sumerian civilisation's development.

In general, An has always been considered to be a bit distant from ordinary people and their needs. As the supreme ruler, An had his own important issues to be concerned about.

In the course of time, An had become a relatively obscure persona within the Sumerian religion. The writings of later times such as hymns and myths are not often mentioning An, since his role is taken over by the Enlil.

Enlil is the 2nd god in the trio of Sumerian gods supreme. The etymology behind his name has sparked a few controversy over the centuries. The most popular interpretation of the name today is to translate that his name means "god from the wind." This interpretation also works with the idea of a vertical order for Sumerian gods, the supreme gods: An (heavens), Enlil (wind, atmoshpere) and Enki (earth).

There is no evidence to suggest that Enlil had been the largest and strong Sumerian god. Many ancient texts mention Enlil in terms of "king over all land", "The Great Mountain" and even "Father of Gods."

It is evident that Enlil and An have the same epithets, which are found in various scripts from the past. It's not certain whether they were ruling together, Enlil was inherited by An (who served as his father) as the god of supreme power or if there was a different story about his ascendance to the position of power. Whatever the case and it is clear that the most important people of those in the Sumerian society, including the kings and rulers, looked to Enlil to confirm their assertions of the power. He himself speaks the name of the king, and gives him the scepter as an indication of his respect and appreciation.

He has the power to make and to destroy. He holds the tablet of destiny which grants him ability and right to control the world. However, Enlil is also the source of wealth: he's the one who provides prosperity to the people.

According to legends according to legends, he provided the human race with the plow and pickax to aid farmers in their efforts. He devised strategies to bring every plant, tree and seeds back to the earth. Contrary to what is commonly believed He was not the demon who would always devise evil plans and caused harm to humans.

The reasoning behind this myth isn't difficult to comprehend However, the reason is not difficult to understand. When we look at the oldest Sumerian writings, it is possible to observe that Enlil had a gruelling job, assigned by gods of other gods to bring about destruction and misery whenever it was believed to be necessary. Therefore, his actions of destruction weren't the result of his bad character however, they were the result of his unremorseful position as a god in the Pantheon. One could argue that this is"him" or his "me."

The most important place of worship in Enlil used to be "e-kur", "Mountain House" situated at Nippur. In the vicinity is a ziggurat constructed by Ur-Namma. Another ziggurat dedicated to the wind's good were found within Assur, Babylon, Dur-Kurigalzu and possibly in Elam which is outside of Mesopotamia.

Enki (Ea) Is the ultimate god of the trinity of gods. His home is an underwater ocean beneath the earth which is called"the "abzu." God of magic and wisdom He is also depicted as a sexual creature, well-known as a fertility god.

According to the ancient myths of creation, Enki is the one responsible for the creation of human beings. He created them out of clay and wanted them to be the ones to do the work, not gods. Enlil was not happy with the creation of his brother because the constant noise kept his sleep. He devised a plan eliminate humanity by creating a massive flood on the earth, causing them to be destroyed.

In the wisdom of his time, Enki was aware of Enlil's plans and was able to have a sage named Atrahasis create an ark to help humans if the flood came upon. This was the reason why human race was spared.

He was also believed to be the god of the land and numerous Sumerian texts speak of his contribution to fertilizing the soil and making it suitable for cultivation and thereby assisting in the creation of settlements that later became huge cities.

The principal place of worship of Enki is the town of Eridu which is located in the southeastern region of Mesopotamia.

Ninhursag (or Ninmah) was another important god of the Sumerian Pantheon, in addition to the three gods that are supreme. She was the mother goddess of all creation goddess of fertility, as well as sacred mountains.

The earliest Sumerian myths indicate that she was in an even higher rank in the hierarchy of gods in the beginning, since her name is frequently mentioned prior to that of Enki.

Ninhursag is usually depicted with the horned cap with mace. In some images she's even accompanied by a wild bear cub that is on a leash. Her name literally translates to"the "Lady of the Mountain" or "the noble lady."

Her symbol, which is akin to that of the Greek omega (albeit it was created earlier than it was incorporated into the Greek alphabet) can be found in a variety of places following 3000 BC. Ninhursag's temple was situated on the Mount Eridu as well as she was also worshipped within the city in Kish in the province of Kish and Lagash.

Nannu God of moonlight was the protector of Ur. Ur. The most well-preserved ziggurat up to date was his site to worship. He played a significant role and influence on The Sumerian religion.

Nannu's most prominent image was of a bull which ties the god to fertility worship as well as in relation to menstrual cycles (moon's changes). In writing, he is depicted as having the appearance of the celestial body: glowing and shining. Moon's movement and transformations were a major factor in the early civilizations, because they were used to determine prophecies and omens. This made Nannu an important major gods that determined the destiny of human race.

In addition to Ur, the Ur city Ur Moon-god was worshipped in Ga'esh close to Ur and Urum. Aside from Mesopotamia, Ur was also worshipped in Harran.

Inanna is among the most intricate Sumerian gods. In some instances, her image depicts a young girl undergoing the influence of a strong patriarchal system, but at other times she is depicted as a feisty goddess who is looking to increase her influence.

Also, her sexuality gets depicted in different ways in poems and written works. In the myth of "Inanna's Descent to the Netherworld," she is very conscious of the traditions and appropriate behavior when it comes to marriage and sexual sex. in the "Epic Of Gilgamesh," on the contrary, she is depicted as a woman fatal who is open to seeking love and, as per Gilgamesh and her refusal to accept her advances and destroys them once she's done with them.

There was another aspect of Inanna also, but not always completely distinct. She was enthusiastic about fighting and war in the military, which highlighted her masculine characteristics.

The "sacred wedding" ceremony that was held during the New Year's celebrations celebrated Inanna's wedding to Dumuzi, the god of the food and plants. Inanna had her own high priestess, while the king performed the role of Dumuzi. The ceremony, used in the 3rd and the 2nd millennium BC helped establish a direct connection with the royal family and realm of the gods.

Inanna's primary shrine was in Uruk, the city she worshipped. Uruk. In addition, as with the other major gods Inanna had temples in several Sumerian cities, including Adab, Girsu, Babylon, Larsa and Ur.

Marduk is a fascinating god who first gained prominence during the middle of the millennium BC. As the patron god of Babylon his influence grew as did his control over the city.

Marduk's ascension is explained as a climax in "The Babylon Epic of Creation." It is in the epic that Marduk fights against the goddess Tiamat who is commonly thought of as the feminine principle. He wins and, after killing the goddess his body is used to make the world. Other gods are thankful to Marduk and, as a token of their appreciation they bestow on Marduk fifty names and select the supreme ruler of their gods. In this way, he takes over

Enlil who was the chief god's ruler at the time.

Like Enlil, Marduk is extremely influential and holds the destiny of the entire creation as well as all gods in his control. He can bring wealth or destruction. He can be simultaneously good and evil.

Outside of his primary location of worship being in Babylon (ziggurat Etemenanki), Marduk was also recognized at Borsippa, Nippur, and Sippar. The Ziggurat Etemenanki is the name which means "temple which is the basis that is the foundation of Heavens as well as Earth" was used as the model for the famed Babel Tower in the Bible. Tower of Babel.

There are a handful of the gods that are mentioned in Sumerian myths, hymns and laments. The task of listing the gods and their functions could be a daunting task, not least because most of them were replaced by others that performed the same functions with an entirely different name (like the instance in the case of Marduk).

Let's now focus on Sumerian rituals to understand the way that people from Sumer considered their role in the world and how they conceived of concepts such as death and life.

Rituals

As we've mentioned, Sumerians believed that men were created from clay for the sole purpose of serving their gods and to make their lives more pleasant as well as more pleasant.

Human beings are nothing more than the slaves of gods and their needs, their fate is never clear. The notion of predetermination as well as total helplessness in the presence of gods is prevalent in their theology and philosophy. Man is predestined for death, and upon his passing is transported to the afterlife realm, which is a dark, dark place in which he is thinking about his life on earth. The eternal bliss and immortality was reserved only for gods.

In accordance with what they believed gods would want to receive from them Sumerians founded their community with the help of laws and law. They were awed by compassion, truthfulness and compassion, avoiding from injustice, deceit and other vices.

Of course the Sumerian religion didn't escape the dilemma of evil and sin as do many other religions that followed. In the Gods' world, they were advocates of morality and goodness as well as morality, were also the ones who brought about the violent and evil. According to the strict definition of "me," there are gods who are responsible to control things such as terror or falsehood.

Then, why gods created all these sinister functions and allow them to exist throughout the world, if they perceive them as being in opposition to all they stand for? It is not surprising that there isn't a single answer to this question found within the Sumerian writings. It was accepted as-is and acknowledged the reality that god's thinking was out of their reach.

The human being must take this for granted as fact however, if is guilty of a sin the only way to get their forgiveness is to pray to God and beg forgiveness. However, the idea for prayer within the early Sumer was very different to what we see in the later religions. As we've said, their primary gods were too distant and busy to listen to the personal pleadings of their followers and so directly begging gods was futile. Each family, however, had their own god, a lesser god who they could turn to every moment of the day. It was their intermediary, and also their representative in the Pantheon.

In the case of burial rituals, they remain a bit hazy until today. From various burial grounds of the royal Sumerian period, it's obvious that kings were interred with their most prized items. The question that isn't as certain however, is whether it was commonplace to have a human retinue with them those who died to their final resting place. The tombs discovered at Ur appear to indicate that this was the case however, the written documents of the time do not confirm the claims. The only piece of written evidence that supports this assertion is a small tablet that contains the last 42 lines from Epic of Gilgamesh, where it is said that Gilgamesh offers offerings to gods of the Nether world in the name of all those who "lay in his presence."

The ordinary mortals were judged in the nether realm in the nether world by Sun God Utu along with Nanna, the Moon goddess Nanna. In order to ease to determine the destiny of people that passed into the nether realm Gods, both personal and gods from the cities were invoked as mediators for them.

The best knowledge we have on the afterlife is derived directly from the text "Gilgamesh, Enkidu, and the Nether World." The way to the final resting spot for the dead was in Erech. A few mortals are permitted to enter the nether realm however they were required adhere to strict rules, including not wearing clean clothing or carry weapons or make any noise and not behave as normal towards the members of the family who resided there in addition to other rules. If one or all of the rules above were violated, the person will be forever in the realm of shadows and would not be allowed for return (unless one gods appealed to for him).

The nether world was ordered according to a system of hierarchy identical to that which existed above the earth. The top positions were held by high priests and dead kings. While it was an unpleasant and dark place however, Sumerian theology suggests that at the evening, the sun will descend into the realm for the deceased, which would make it more luminous.

Living, even though they had their own gods but the main place of worship in each metropolis is in the shrine (ziggurat). There were many temples scattered across Sumer that were dedicated to the important and minor gods. Enki was the name of his shrine. Eridu the most famous Temple of An was discovered in Erech. The temples of the early times served as models for later, more complicated ziggurats.

The construction of temples was supported by numerous rituals and ceremonies. When they were built, they functioned as a venue where daily ceremonies took place. Priests offered sacrifices, usually vegetables and animals and also wine, beer and water. There were many festivals or feasts during which the rituals became more festive with specific sacrifices and rituals.

It was believed that the New Year holiday was, probably the most significant of all. It was observed over a time of seven days, and was commemorated by the previously described ceremony of "holy wedding" between the King along with the high priests associated with the Goddess Innanna.

We have no information about the priests that were responsible for the temple. We do know that the administrator of the temple was referred to in the form of the "sang." He was the one responsible for overseeing the temple as well as ensuring that each member was performing their tasks and finances were in good condition. "En" served as the leader of the temple who could be male or female. The gender of "en" was generally determined by the god's sex who the temple was dedicated.

For Sumerians who lived in the Sumerians, the worst calamity that could happen to an entire city was the devastation of the temple. This is logical considering the significance the temple had in their daily lives and also the fact that they considered the temple to be the place where they could worship their god of patronage.

Mythology

The ancient myths, though stuffed with fairytales and legends they often provide an glimpse into the lives of the ancient civilizations. Sumerian myths provide a wealth of details about their beliefs and worldviews that aid in understanding their motives for different actions and endeavors.

The myths are primarily centered around the birth of gods and their most important moments in their lives, as well as the actions by which they confer blessings and curses. In contrast to other stories, Sumerian texts rarely discuss conflicts between gods and, however, when conflicts do happen they are not described as bloody, fierce fights to the end rather, they are described as smaller, more subdued conflicts.

The origin of everything

The story of creation is a central part of numerous cultures of the past. But, we don't discover such a story from The

Sumerian writings. The concepts of creation of the world are discussed in various songs and poems, but an original piece of writing specifically with this subject hasn't been discovered.

Beyond the origins of the universe There are numerous myths that address various other important elements that concern the organization for the creation of all things, development of human beings, and finally the creation of civilization. The gods who play the leading part of these stories are generally Enlil, Enki, Ninhursag, Nanna, Ninurta (the god of the south the wind), Martu, and Inanna.

The legend "Enlil And"the Creation of the Pickax," the god of supreme power, separated heaven from earth and created the seeds of different plants, and then presented the pickax to Sumerians. Thus, even though there's no explanation of the exact way in which heaven earth, heaven, and gods were created but the majority of what happened since the moment of creation can be attributed to Enlil.

The exile of Enlil to the realm of the dead

Sumerian gods could be powerful however they weren't completely at liberty to rule however they wanted. Even the god of supreme power, Enlil, was once penalized for his transgressions, and was banished to the nether realm.

According to the legend according to the legend, goddess Ninlil was commanded by mother Nunbarshegunu to swim naked in the stream to try to seduce Enlil. The God recognizes Ninlil with her splendor and is drawn to her. But his attraction is so strong that it is impossible for him to wait for actions to take place right in the way that Ninlil's mother believed.

Enlil enters the boat, gets close to Ninlil and she snatches her away despite Ninlil's protests. In the end, she has a son born named who is the Moon God Sin.

The remainder part of the Pantheon is horrified by the actions of Enlil, and decides that he should be punished for his immoral acts. In spite of his position as King and leader of the Pantheon, he is arrested and sent to the abyss of the world.

The God is willing to accept his punishment because there's nothing other he can do, however Ninlil who is expecting her child, is determined in her determination to join him in the realm of the underworld. This is not a pleasant thought for Enlil as she does not want his son to be raised in the dark world.

Since the goddess can't be dissuaded, the Enlil chooses an alternative method. He transforms into three minor gods that all of us encounter on our way to the realm of the dead. He imbibes Ninlil three times more and creates three new gods to fill the role of Sin who is in the lower realms to allow him to go to heaven where he belongs.

This is the curse that Ninhursag has suffered.

The curse that Ninhursag imposes on God Enki is the main theme of another well-known Sumerian myth. It is set in the region of Dilmun which is a clear and shining, where there isn't any death or illness.

In this location, Ninhursag manages to bring eight unique plants to life. According to the myth, it was an extremely complex process that required a lot of effort on the part of Ninhursag. Enki is completely unaware of the situation, orders his god of messengers Ismud to pounce on the plants and deliver the plants to him for tasting. After discovering this the goddess is angry and curses death on Enki and then disappears to show that she is not changing her choice.

Enki becomes sick and, symbolically eight of his organs become affected. Other gods cannot assist him, even his brother, the great Enlil. In the midst of despair the fox comes to his rescue with the promise that he can restore Ninhursag back, provided that the gods bless him (the Fox) in a proper manner. The deal is made and the fox fulfills his word. What exactly does the fox do however, isn't known. The texts that describe this part of the legend are not available therefore we have to guess. But, the goddess appears and has pity on Enki.

The process of healing is yet again, a complex one. In order to heal all eight organs She creates eight distinct healing gods who work to bring Enki back to full health.

The story is full of connections to the biblical tale of the Garden of Eden and the creation of Eve from Adam's rib. In the story of Enki one of his organs in a state of sickness was his the rib ("ti").

The creation of men

Enki is the main character in a second important Sumerian mythology: the beginning of humankind. Gods complain about their inability to procure their food, and Enki is God of Wisdom is asked to provide the solution.

To please gods Enki makes human creatures out of clay and then gives them the ability to perform the tasks instead of gods. The tale of how humans were created is told in a couple of verses which is in keeping with the way Sumerians generally expressed their beliefs about their gods. Enki desired to create a god, and it did happen.

The remainder of the poem explains the development of six flawed kinds humans. When Enki and Ninhursag feast in celebration of Enki's most recent piece, her goddess creates six individuals who are not normal. The God attempts to create the one of his own however, he fails. His creature is incompetent and weak, and unable to even survive by itself. To remedy this Ninhursag curses Enki and is willing to accept the curse as punishment for his error.

Inanna's descent to the Nether World

The goddess Inanna (or Ishtar) is mentioned in numerous Sumerian myths. This particular myth is most well-known as it describes how this ardent goddess of war and love is able to go into the underworld to claim her own place in the universe.

Goddess Ereshkigal serves as her sister and head of the Netherworld. Inanna is afraid that her sibling may be doing once she is in her domain, therefore she tells Ninshubur her vizier that if she doesn't come returning in 3 days, she must begin to scream at the altar of the Gods. In the next three days, he'll have to take her to plead her case before Enlil to get her back. If that doesn't work, Ninshubur should visit Nanna and ask the same thing. In the event that his pleas do not fall in the ear of these gods, he must visit Enki God of wisdom.

Once the preparations are completed after which she travels into the gates of underworld the world in elegant clothes and sporting beautiful jewelry. Innana is able to trick the gatekeeper (or as she believes) to let her in and, as they go through seven gates leading to in the realm of darkness, her possessions of jewelry and clothing are taken away in pieces. At the point she is able to reach her mother and Anunnaki (seven judges from the realm of the dead) the woman is completely naked. The fears of her be justified as she is instantly transformed into a corpse before being hanged on an upright.

In the wake of his mistress not returning, Ninshubur sets upon fulfilling Inanna's wish in the fourth day. Enki will be the one willing to help, so Ninshubur comes up with an idea to rescue Inanna from being swept into the clutches of the realm of the nebulous. He makes two sexless creatures and then sends these to Ereshkigal. They are carrying"the water of life" and "water that lives" as well as"food of life. "food from life."

The creatures must feel empathy for Ereshkigal who is sick. once they have won her affection they will be given the gift of grain and water. They should decline these presents and instead, demand the lifeless body hanging from the ceiling. When she has given her the corpse of Innana the next step is allowed to sprinkle the body with liquids and food that life has and return it to life.

The plan works , and Innana is brought back However, she has to find a new person to join her in the etheric world. That was the way it is, and she was not the only exception. Numerous demons follow them back down to earth should she fail to locate a replacement, they'll return.

Because Inanna was a deity she is able to be replaced by another god. Inanna begins her search for the perfect replacement. Upon reaching the town of Erech that is run by her husband the shepherd god Dumuzi, she discovers him praising her misfortunes instead of mourning her departure. The goddess is unhappy, and she tells the demons to bring her husband to the underworld world, instead of her.

Afraid of the possibility of being a victim, he appeals to his Sun god Utu Inanna's brother to protect him from the dreadful fate awaiting him. Utu attempts to intervene, however Innana is ruthless and Dumuzi is taken into the underworld, where he will endure the punishment of Inanna.

There are many intriguing Sumerian myths available. Many of them are incomplete while others, such as the tale about Inanna as well as Dumuzi were made complete due to other sources than the original source. These myths and others provide us with a glimpse into the beliefs of the Sumerian man. His gods were over him, and they were his slaves However, they weren't flawless, invincible creatures. They also were required to observe the rules and follow the laws, or face the punishment was imposed. If this was the plan of gods, how can a person protest?

Chapter 3: Lighter Tales of Sumerian Gods and Heroes

Sumerian heroes are fascinating due to the fact that many of them such as Gilgamesh and Atrahasis were real people who were King before entering the realm of mythology. According to the Epic of Gilgamesh, especially the formal epic written many centuries after the epic poems (which were the basis for the original material), Gilgamesh is described as a half-man and half-god. This means that Gilgamesh basically a god on the same level as several heroes from the Greeks.

It is interesting to consider the role of the demigod within Sumerian mythology as an early precursor to two distinct stories about Sumerian heroes, specifically tales that revolve around heroes like Lugulbanda. Demigods are essentially people who is not a god, but rather more than a human. The place of the demigod within the canonical mythology of Sumer is very similar to the role of the demigod in the Greeks but the latter was considered as a character that had distinct particular identity. According to them, the demigod had the status of being the son of gods or goddess who was the mortal. In the same way that the Greeks believed in that the divine lineage significant and important, the Sumerians considered those who were great as elevated to semi-godly status through because of their heroic acts. This isn't much different. Sure, great dynasties and kings from Greek areas must have believed that they had the gods of their ancestors to justify their status. Therefore, when the Sumerians were pragmatic about their position - just placing their great men in the same category in stature and status to gods - it appears to be that the Greeks altered the course of history and claimed their greatest rulers were actually gods' sons and, therefore, real demigods and not just ordinary mortals.

Lugalbanda located in the Mountain Cave

Lugalbanda is an excellent illustration of Lugalbanda, the Sumerian demigod. Although he's listed as an actual person specifically the second King in the city of Uruk and was believed to have ruled over 1200 years. This isn't at all in line with the mortals. In this regard, the Sumerian ruler is akin to the kinds of legends about Egyptian pharaohs. Many of whom were believed to have lived for more than 100 years old. It's been difficult to find out the truth of this claim. Lugalbanda actually was a living person, however the evidence suggests that Sumerians believed that he was real. He was included in their lists of kings at the very least.

Lugalbanda at The Mountain Cave is a story that is sometimes referred to in the form of Lugalbanda to the Wilderness. This tale and other stories about Lugalbanda are part of a certain mythology that is about the conflict between a king called Enmerkar and a different King who was the ruler of Aratta. Aratta. The tale is very old, dating from around 2100 BC however, the tablets we have today date approximately 300 years after.

The story starts with Enmerkar making his way through Aratta, the capital city. Aratta as the leader of a huge army. His soldiers include Lugalbanda. For the warrior Lugalbanda, he gets sick and his brothers abandon him in the cave. It's dependent on the gods if the warrior survives or dies. Lugalbanda prays to a variety of gods, including Inanna,

Shamash, and Nanna. He prays for the healing of the disease that caused him to be ill. Gods respond to his prayers and, eventually, Lugalbanda is able to escape the cave. Lugalbanda hunts a bull as well as two wild goats before lying down to sleep to
dream. Lugalbanda dreams that it is instructed to sacrifice the animals to gods as a sacrifice. Lugalbanda awakes and performs the act as the dream has told him. Even though the remainder of the story has been obscured by time of many thousands of years, the story appears to illustrate both the natures of gods, who are both powerful and occasionally cruel.

Lugalbanda as well as Lugalbanda and Anzu Bird

Lugalbanda and Lugalbanda and Anzu bird tells a tale that continues Lugalband within The Wilderness (or Lugalbanda in the Mountain Cave) in sequence. The tale is also part of the series of tales that feature Enmerkar fighting the kingdom (whose name is now lost) from Aratta. As with the other story the one that follows was written around 2100 BC with the other records of it dating back to around 1800 BC.

Lugalbanda's story as well as the Anzu birds begins by a hero who is traveling through the hills. He comes across the newly hatched chicks that belongs to Anzu, the Anzu bird. We've seen this bird previously, but it's basically a huge eagle that has the head of the Lion. Lugalbanda feeds the chick when its mother is away. After the Anzu bird comes back, it is surprised that the chick has failed to respond to the signal. It discovers that Lugalbanda was tending to the chick, and decides to honor the hero. The Anzu bird gives Lugalbanda an ability to cover great distances in a brief amount of time. Similar to superman's power to "leap high buildings in one go," et cetera.

With his new skills with him, Lugalbanda returns to his King Enmerkar who continues to lay the siege on Aratta but is having a lot of difficulties with this task. Enmerkar would like to visit Inanna to beg her for help during the siege. Lugalbanda agrees the opportunity to travel and can accomplish quickly due to the power that he was granted from his Anzu bird. When he arrives at Inanna, Lugalbanda is given instructions regarding how the army will overpower the Aratta city. Aratta.

Chapter 4: Akkadian Empire and Mythology

It was the first state of Mesopotamia was the one belonging to the Akkadians. Their state dates back to around 2334 BC up to 2194 BC. The Akkadian Empire encompassed Sumer itself and also regions in the north. It covered most of the present-day Iraq as well as areas from Turkey, Syria, and Kuwait. Akkad was significant, not just as the first kingdom that we know about however, it was also important in terms of its art of architecture, the religion as well as the advancements exported to other areas. The chapter that follows we'll increase our understanding about Sumerian society and its religion by exploring what some think of as the most important point of Sumerian achievements in terms of culture and politics that is The Akkadian Empire. We will explore the life that of the greatest King of Mesopotamia - Sargon, the King. Sargon and look into the details and the stories that create the Akkadian period fascinating even if it is a less well-known one.

Sargon of Akkad

Akkad used to be the name given to the city as well as the region. It is crucial to keep in mind that during the early days of Mesopotamia and, later on cities were at the heart of politics and religion. City-states were the primary political system of Mesopotamia and was to remain so over the course of millennia. However rising empires such as that of Akkadian, Babylonian, and Assyrian might alter the emphasis on the city-state. In this way, Sumerian history does seem to have a resemblance to the later Greek historical events. In Greece as well the city-state's political unit later gave way to bigger empires and kingdoms like the one of Macedon and the Seleucids.

Sargon was therefore born into a complex and tangled political web that was comprised of independent city-states and non-Sumerian populations living close of the Sumerians. For instance it is believed that the term Akkad is not a Sumerian name that would suggest that at the very least, one or two of the people living who lived in Mesopotamia in the present and not just the Akkadians themselves were not just Sumerian but maybe not Mesopotamian. Akkad was a city in the region of Akkad was situated in the plain that was between two rivers, the Tigris as well as the Euphrates rivers, though the exact location of the city has not been confirmed.

Sargon established his reign by destroying his city state of Uruk that was ruled by a ruler known as Lugal-zage si. Lugal-zage-si is believed by many to be the only king from Uruk's Third Dynasty of Uruk, which was possibly the most important of Sumerian city-states of the time. Sargon took over Lugal-zage-si's state which included smaller cities.

Sargon himself was born of humble ancestry. Sargon his name, which translates to "the legitimate King" was the son of a gardener named Itti-Bel, or La'ibum. It was said that his mother's mother had been an hierodule for Inanna, the Goddess. Inanna (or Ishtar). Hierodules were sacred prostitute who was a goddess's servant in various ways within her temple. Another legend says the Sargon's mom was mute while Sargon did not have a father. According to this legend, Sargon's mother was pregnant and placed Sargon in a basket before took him to the river. Sargon was rescued by a man whose work was to draw out the waters. The man who raised him bred Sargon and eventually made Sargon his gardener. Sargon's genealogy was later expanded to give his ancestors an appearance of nobleness and a status they had previously not had in the earlier sources.

We know that Sargon began his career as a cupbearer for the King of Kish which was a major city-state. The king was named Ur-Zababa. Sargon then succeeded him as a cupbearer. In actual fact, the role of the cupbearer was believed to be important in the period as it put the holder close to the King. Sargon was to rule for 45 years, in accordance with a Cuneiform version. Most people believe that he actually ruled during 56 years. In this period the king greatly expanded his kingdom. For instance Sargon, the King Sargon was a conqueror that was Canaan as well as Syria 4 times.

The greatest achievement of Sargon was his unification of two city states of Sumer as well as Akkad to the very first time. This turned Mesopotamia to become a major economic and political center that had no rivals. Trade was flourishing in the region. The silver of Asia Minor and cedar from Lebanon were traded along with lapis-lazuli from mountains of present-day Afghanistan along with copper from Phoenicia. The mainstay for the economic system was agricultural products from Assyria located just to North of Sumer.

The monumental representations of Sargon were built across Mesopotamia as well as on the eastern shores of Mediterranean Sea. Sargon expanded his power over Mesopotamia and into the Eastern Mediterranean. Sargon conquered the areas of Elam as well as Subartu. In the documents were compiled to document his achievements (on his memorials), Sargon boasted of conquering the four quarters of the region, which comprised Sumer, Assyria, Elam and Martu. It is believed that Sargon rebuilt Babylon, the city that was Babylon even though it could be a tiny settlement in the present.

Unity of Akkadians and Sumerians

As regards religion in terms of religion, in terms of religion, the Sargonic time was also a time of unified religion in many ways. Of of course both the Sumerians and Akkadians found themselves united politically and also began an age of religious and cultural syncretism that would last for many centuries. This would be so extensive that, eventually Sumerian was to be substituted with Akkadian and other languages that were not Sumerian. However, Sargon was wise enough to not alienate the Sumerian people who were religious. He was particularly concerned about paying tribute to Zababa and Inanna as they were the two gods that were important to the Sumerians. Inanna was a highly revered queen of heaven , and also the patron goddess of Sargon and Zababa, while Zababa was the god of war from the town of Kish.

The process of unification initiated by Sargon would be a source of difficulties. These problems arose both in Sargon's personal existence as well as the time of the successors to him. A number of King revolted against Sargon and formed coalitions. Sargon had a lot of success beating his adversaries repeatedly and again during his life. Rimush And Manishtushu were the sons of Sargon who were kings following Sargon's death. Both were forced to fight against rebels seeking to take down the empire that their father constructed. The Akkadian Empire saw a revival in the form of a revival under the reign of the son of Manishtushi Naram-Sin. He overcame his revivals and continued the process of economic, religious and political unification that was happening in Mesopotamia. It was about 100 years after the death of Naram-Sin to the point that the Akkadian Empire would fall which would bring in the dark ages of Mesopotamia. In the meantime the governance of the region was those of city-states that competed with each other for influence.

Martu's Marriage Marriage of Martu

The Marriage of Martu is a story from the Akkadian period, or the period immediately following. It is believed to date back to the time between 2200 BC between 2200 BC and 2000 BC. The story tells of Martu and his relationship with an enchanting princess. Martu was a different name for Amurru who was later to become the patron god for the Amorites who established the

Babylonian Empire. In the tale, Martu is described as an armed warrior. It was not unusual to see gods in these earlier stories to appear as normal people, even although they were worshipped by the devotees of the region.

Martu is in the city to find an ideal bride for him. He is able to see a gorgeous princess, and she notices him as well. He is able to win the heart of the princess by beating the opponent in a wrestling contest. He delights the princess's family by presenting them with gifts. The princess's father offers his approval to this union. A person who observes the wedding points out that Martu is a nomad living outside of the city seems uncivil, but the princess is not concerned about this. There are several significant themes that are explored in The Marriage of Martu. One of it is that love is able to conquer everything, while another is the significant connection between urban dwellers and rural dwellers. It was necessary for both to reach a consensus in order to collaborate to build the empires being built within the area.

Chapter 5: Twenty Vital facts concerning Sumerian History and Mythology

Fact One. Sumerian civilization was the longest known civilization on earth.

Sumer was remarkable, but not only because of its accomplishments. Sumer was unique for its ability to capable of condensing the most impressive achievements of its time in one place and time. The history of Sumer tells us that Sumerians were the first civilization, much older that the Egyptians. As the first civilization they Sumerians were a large urban areas where they constructed magnificent structures called Ziggurats. The early Sumerian cities made significant progress that are still evident until today.

Fact Two. Sumer is located in a significant geographic region , which is known as Mesopotamia.

Mesopotamia is the term used to describe the land that lies between two rivers. Sumer was situated in the southern portion of Mesopotamia it was an extremely fertile area since it was situated between two rivers. The area was well-watered and flat ideal for farming or pasture land. The rivers which the Mesopotamian land is situated in between are the Tigris River and Euphrates River. The majority of Mesopotamia is located in the current nation of Iraq but there are parts of it located in Kuwait, Turkey, and Syria.

Fact Three. Humans' transition from hunter-gatherers to large-scale agricultural activities is believed to take place around Sumer.

It's easy to take civilisation for granted since it has existed for so many years. If you were living in the past, like Sumer and you were a child, you wouldn't take the existence of civilization for granted. You'd have observed all around you the obvious distinction between living in cities and outside of cities. The Sumerians even shared stories of people who experienced firsthand the differences. The primary factor that enabled people to reside in cities was the advancement of large-scale agriculture practices. The change to this type of cultivation was initiated in this area, and is the reason the development of civilization began here too.

Fact Four. The oldest system of writing around the globe was invented in Sumer.

The Sumerians were awash with stories of how the writing process began. One of them involved the king having to manage the numerous messages he needed to exchange with a different king. In reality, the language was developed because urban life required a method to communicate swiftly and efficiently, without having to speak. which could get lost during the recounting.

Fact Five. Numerous common elements of math and timekeeping originate from Sumerians.

The Sumerians are the source of many significant advances in the fields of mathematics and astronomy. The sixty-second minute was one of them and the sixty-minute hour. They also divided each year's calendar into 12 segments similar to what we do today.

Fact Six. The Sumerian pantheon was comprised of between one to 350 gods.

The Sumerians were a religious people who worshipped a lot of gods. There are several intriguing reasons to this. One of them is that every city-state had a patron god whom they built a massive temple to and also there were a number of cities. Another reason is that when cities became empires the gods of different religions were unifying in a pantheon.

Fact Seven. In the course of time, the people of Mesopotamia were merged both in terms of their language and religious practice.

A single of the more fascinating periods of Sumerian historical records is Akkadian. The Akkadian period was notable because of the fusion of two different cultures, that of Akkad and

Sumer. These two groups each had their own gods and languages at this time, and as a result an era of religious and cultural fusion was beginning.

Fact Eight. Many empires occupied the area of Sumer which included those of Akkadian, Hurrian, Babylonian, Assyrian, and Persian.

It is believed that the Mesopotamian region was noted for the multitude of states that built empires upon the fertile plain. While certain states were from outside but not all were. For instance those of the Akkadian, Assyrian, and Babylonian empires are able to be described to be Mesopotamian states.

Fact Nine. The first political system in Sumer comprised city-states that were independent.

It was believed that the city-state formed the primary political structure of Sumer. It is logical since city life is a part of civilization and it is essential to begin with cities before progressing to the level of empires. And even after thousands of years cities remained the main basis of the political system in Mesopotamia.

Fact Ten. There is a belief that a lot characters from Sumer such as Gilgamesh, Lugalbanda, and Atrahasis were kings of the past.

The most interesting thing in mythology is the fact that typically, the mythical heroes were real individuals. Historical scholars think they believe that Gilgamesh, Lugalbanda, and Atrahasis were real kings that resided in Sumer. Sargon is another instance of a king who's life was hidden by legend.

Fact Eleven. Sumerian mythology and culture have the greatest similarities in common with Norse in terms of the major belief systems.

The Norse were another group of people who emphasized historiography and heroes and tales of men and gods. In fact the Norse sagas are in fact stories of heroes, many of them were real men. In this sense, Sumer has quite a number of things in common with the Norse. It is also possible to say that the Sumerians share a few similarities with the Greeks as well. The Greeks also put much importance on heroes, but the line that separated god and hero was quite distinct in Greek mythology and not than with the Sumerians.

Fact Twelve. The status of godhead of the Sumerian pantheon was changed with time.

One of the interesting facts concerning one of the most interesting aspects about Sumerians was that they didn't have a god who was stable throughout their time. Their main god was Enlil or Anu, and sometimes the god was Enlil or Anu or Anu, but at there were times when they had Marduk Ashur, Nanna, or Inanna. This is a unique event in time, but it is a reflection of the reality of Sumerian political system and the changing status of Mesopotamia as a ruler. Each city had its god, and as one city grew, so the god of that city. This pattern continued to be replicated as empires took over cities-states. When an empire grew in power, it was promoting their own God.

Fact Thirteen. Every empire that was part of Mesopotamia had a new chief god in comparison to the one that was before it.

The Babylonians were known to have Marduk as god The Assyrians were devoted to their god Ashur. They replaced the previous gods, the chief gods, like Enlil and An which had played a significant role in the region.

Fact Fourteen. The gods from Sumer was believed to descend to An (or Anu) who was the god of the sky.

Gods from Sumer were often known as the Anunnaki. The pantheon was a reflection of how they derived from gods of the sky (or celestial bodies), An. It was believed that the Sumerians believed that the beginning of life came with cosmic births. God Enlil was the god of sky An And the earth was Ki. Enlil later overtook Ki to become the god of the earth.

Fact 15. Inanna was the longest-lived in the history of Sumerian gods and was revered up to the 18th century.

Inanna truly was an intriguing goddess. She was referred to as the Queen of Heaven and Lady of Earth. She was the daughter to the god of the Underworld goddess, Ereshkigal. Most importantly, Inanna was also the goddess of love as well as a god of war. Inanna must have had an appeal if she lived the length of time she did, literally beating all other gods.

Fact Sixteen. Inanna was introduced to Greek mythology under the name Aphrodite.

Greek historians were aware that Aphrodite was not a goddess of their people. Aphrodite had arrived with people of the Greeks as Ashtoreth as an ancient Phoenician goddess. She had travelled through trade with Phoenician (and Greek ports). However, Ashtoreth was not a different goddess than Inanna or Ishtar an ancient strong and potent Sumerian goddess.

Fact Seventeen. Lugalbanda was one of the kings from Sumer who is believed to have ruled for over 1200 years.

The distinction between god and hero was somewhat blurred in Sumerian mythology. Sumerian stories tell of kings who sometimes asked to be ordained as gods. They were typically denied however that didn't hinder them from ruling for hundreds of years like if

they had been gods. Lugalbanda is a
great illustration of this.

Fact Eighteen. The Sumerian thirst for
beer was represented in a god of theirs
named Ninkasi the goddess of beer.

A lot of Sumerian stories focus on
drinking beer or about a certain
person's affinity for beer. In fact, it is
not a surprise to learn that Sumerians
had the god of beer, Ninkasi. A lot of
Sumerian myths delve into ramblings
about the splendor of a city, or its
magnificent monuments or the grandeur
of temples or the god it was a part
of. Some stories even begin to talk
about beer. It's a mystery.

Fact Nineteen. The Sumerians wrote in
cuneiform for over three thousand
years, up to the period of Jesus.

What's interesting about Sumerian
writing in cuneiform is the fact that they
continued to use it, as well as variations
of it, to at the close of civilisation. This
was even when new ways of writing that
could be easier to use were
invented. This isn't difficult to
comprehend when one bears in mind
the importance of the religion of writing

and the importance of keeping this sacred writing in its original format.

Fact Twenty. Sumerian historical records were lost approximately 200 years in the past. We are now capable of retracing Sumerian history using the help of 500 000 tablets that have been discovered (some remain been translated).

The ability to decipher clay tablets has helped us to comprehend the Sumerian world with some speed. It's awe-inspiring consider that hundreds of thousands of tablet to be decoded. Imagine the amazing things are there to discover.

A list of Sumerian gods, goddesses and Heroes

It is believed that the Sumerian pantheon was awash with gods and goddesses, demons and monsters that numbered more than 3000 in number. A number of gods were synthesized over time, or their names change. For instance, Inanna saw her cult expand rapidly over time and was referred to in the form of Ishtar within Babylon as well as Ashtoreth within Phoenicia. The main gods in The Sumerians changed. At one time it was Enlil and at another time, An as well as at other times, Ashur or Marduk. In this article, we offer a link to the gods, goddesses and other characters from Sumerian mythology.

Chief Deities:

Enlil (or Ellil): the Great Mountain, Lord of the Wind The Godfather of the Gods

(or An): god of sky. (or An): god of the sky

Enki God of Wisdom water, creation, and wisdom as the god of water, creation, and wisdom; Earth

Other Gods:

Adad: God of Storms

Amurru god of nomads and the Lord of the Mountains God of the Amorites, eponymous god of Amorites

Anzu is a huge bird that steals an entire tablet of destiny. Tablet of Destinies

Apkallu is one of the seven wise men, or wise men of Babylonian myth

Ashur God of Ashur: The god among the Assyrian people, often depicted on an animal

Bull of Heaven: character that appears as a character in The Epic of Gilgamesh; Inanna gets her dad Anu to unleash the Bull of Heaven against Gilgamesh

Ea: God of the seas on the which Earth is floating

Ereshkigal goddess of the underworld, sister to Inanna The Queen of Heaven

Gula Goddess of Doctors and healing

Inanna or Ishtar the goddess of war, love, and fertility

Lama Goddess of private or personal protection (the same as Lamassu however, it is depicted in female form.)

Lamassu is a bull or lion that has an human head

Lamashtu is a demon who preys on children

Mami is a goddess of motherhood of Atrahasis's Epic of Atrahasis

Marduk God of protection for Babylon

Martu: an alternative title for Amurru the god of Amurru, the eponymous god of the Amorites

Mushhushshu A ferocious dragon or snake that acts as the protector of the gods that are not part from the Sumerian pantheon

Nabu Patron writer and deity of the scribes

Nanna God of Wisdom and moon, also called Sin

Nergal god of the underworld; husband of Ereshkigal

Ninhursag: the mother goddess of Sumer

Ninurta: God of War

Nanna God of Wisdom and the moon.

Pazuzu, the god of demons who shields humans from harmful forces and diseases

The Scorpion People are God's servants Shamash (or Utu-Shamash)

Sin: moon god

Tiamat was a goddess of rage who battled against gods which was frequently depicted in the form of an enormous dragon or sea serpent. Tigris as well as the Euphrates flow through her body cut in half

Ugallu is a demon who has the head of an lion, the human body with feet like a bird. safeguards humans from illnesses

Usmu is the messenger god as well as god of Ea, the capital city. Ea

Utu-Shamash (or Shamash): God of the sun; brother of Inanna.

Main Heroes:

Enmerkarwas a king who was believed to have ruled between 425 and 900 years

Etana is the legendary city's king. Kish

Gilgamesh Hero from The Epic of Gilgamesh; also a historical King of Uruk. Uruk.

Utnapishtum is a hero of the epic of Gilgamesh. Epic of Gilgamesh; said to be an ancestor to Gilgamesh

Frequently Answered Questions

1. What were they? Sumerians?

Sumerians Sumerians were the people from Sumer the region of Mesopotamia. Mesopotamia was the region between two rivers, which were the Tigris River and the Euphrates River. This region is primarily in Iraq but there are parts of it as well in Syria, Turkey, and Kuwait. The region was extremely fertile, and the Sumerians resided in the southernmost part of the region. The Sumerians were non-Semitic in their language writing in script called cuneiform which was also non-Semitic in origin.

The location and even the concept of Sumerians changed during the Akkadian period. The Sumerian period was technically 2000 years and started approximately 4000-4500 BC. The Sumerians eventually got replaced by the Akkadians, who lived in the northern part of Sumer. The Sumerian language was forced be able to contend with Akkadian dialect, and this led to the inhabitants who were part of Akkad to be Akkadian Empire (who had control over simultaneously Akkad as well as Sumer) to have to remain largely bilingual.

2. What was important in this period? Sumerian period?

The Sumerians were important because of a variety of factors. In one sense, a lot of the technological advances we take for granted in modern times were developed by the Sumerians. A large portion of our knowledge of astrology, maths and accounting originates directly from Sumerians. They Sumerians divided the minutes into sixty seconds and hours into 60 mins. It was a year divided in twelve divisions of twelve, and utilized the constellations of the sky to determine time and to predict the weather.

The one thing you should learn regarding what happened to the Sumerians and the time their time is the fact that Sumerians are widely believed as the first civilisation that ever existed. In reality, it is stated that they invented the concept of civilized living. Since they were the Masters of Agriculture, the people were no longer required to be sifting for food or addressing other issues of life. Only a small percentage of people could meet the demands for feeding the people, while others could be adapted in other areas. Tradesmen could not exist without the advances in agriculture of the Sumerians. In fact, there would not be mathematicians or researchers without farmers carrying the burden of feeding the masses onto their own shoulders. We have Sumerians to be thankful for this shift in how humans live.

3. Did peoples like the Sumerians along with those of the Akkadians two distinct groups of people?

It's sometimes difficult to determine who the ancient peoples really were or the place they originated from. In particular, until today historians aren't completely sure of what they think the Ancient Egyptians "were" or the place they came from. They used an Semitic language which differed from the different Semitic languages. Did they originate out of in the Near East, Africa, or both? These types of questions are extremely difficult to answer as our understanding of nationality as well as ethnicity is merely that is contemporary. The people from the past weren't as "pure" as the people nowadays like to believe they were in their own group. They were in fact mixed from the diverse peoples that passed across the area.

However this doesn't answer the question regarding how to distinguish between the Sumerians as well as the

Akkadians therefore we'll attempt to answer that question also. There was a time when the Sumerians along with the Akkadians were distinct individuals. The Sumerians had a distinct language that was different from the Akkadians. They lived in remote areas, too although they both Sumer as well as Akkad are part of the country that is Iraq and are no more or less ethnically distinct. A lot has been written about the dual nature of the Akkadian Imperial Period, which is evidence the two communities of Akkad Sumer and Akkad Sumer were initially distinct until political tensions eventually caused an amalgamation between these two people. This was a process that was to remain common across Mesopotamia.

4. What was the most popular language used in the Akkadian period?

In the Akkadian period there were two languages spoken. There was the first Sumerian language, which was distinct from the other because it had its own writing style. There was also the Akkadian language that was a distinct language that had its own distinct style of writing. Because Akkadian was not able to replace Sumerian in the beginning because of the cultural and religious significance of Sumerian and its people, many in the past would have had a bilingual status in Sumerian and Akkadian or at least that is what historians of the present believe. As the gods and the cultures were merged, Sumerian as a language would fade away.

5. Which were Amorites and what was their significance?

The Amorites were an Semitic people, whose land was beyond Mesopotamia. Particularly, they lived in their own "steppes" and mountainside to the west of Sumer which is why they were located in the Eastern Mediterranean Sea. The Amorites have been influenced by theorists who had different agendas throughout the centuries, but now we are aware that they were a Semitic people, possibly similar to the Canaanites who lived throughout the Southern Levant before the arrival of the Jews from Egypt.

Amurru used to be the term used for two distinct group of people (who we today recognize in the form of Amorites) and also for the god they revered. The god they worshipped was named Martu and his significant city was known as Ninab. Like other cities of this region, the exact place of this city is unknown to archaeologists and historians. Amurru as well as Martu are mentioned in texts from both Akkadian and Sumerian languages.

Amurru was considered to be God of the Amorite people. The Amorites were originally people of the tribal and uncivilized that lived in the margins of both the Akkadian as well as the Neo-Sumerian empires. They were pastoralists, and were frequently referred to as being of the mountain or the steppe. This is why Amurru (the God of the gods) was also known as the Lord of the Mountain or the lord of the steppe.

6. What was the principal god for the Sumerians?

It's not an easy question to be answered. In fact, it's an even more difficult question in the case of the Sumerians than it is for Greeks, Romans, or the Norse. The Greeks were home to Zeus as well as the Norse were ruled by Odin. It's that simple. However, for the Sumerians the gods of the main religion were changed according to the rulers who were in charge in the city at considered to be the central point of the civilization.

Enlil is often thought of as the main Sumerian god, however that's only true for the early times of Sumer along with in the Akkadian period. In the past gods such as An or Enki even matched Enlil in terms of importance, or exceeded Enlil in importance or even surpassed him. For the Assyrians, and during the Assyrian period of Sumer, Ashur was the god of the highest rank. In this Babylonian time, Sumer's most powerful god was Marduk. In time, Inanna grew in importance to become one of the gods most worshipped in Mesopotamia. As you can see, Mesopotamians didn't really have an Zeus or Odin who held a stifling position in their culture. The pantheon they had was constantly changing to accommodate new gods and their principal god was modified to the rulers who were in charge of Sumer and their principal city (and divinity) was.

7. Are Mesopotamian divinities mentioned in the area of Mesopotamia?

There were a number of Sumerian divinities were mentioned in the documents of the neighboring regions. In certain instances they were believed to the gods in these regions, whereas in other cases, they were described as having a conflict against local gods and people. For instance The Bible and Talmud contain references to many gods from other countries that include Sumerian gods. Ba'al, for instance, was the name of an ancient Canaanite god, however his name only was "lord" and many Mesopotamian gods may be compared to Ba'al. Nergal is a fascinating god because of the references to him in other places than Mesopotamia.

Nergal was the god of the lower world. He was portrayed in numerous myths as the wife of Ereshkigal who was the supreme ruler of the underworld as well as the wife of Inanna The goddess of Heaven. Nergal's place of worship was located in his city, Cuthah and was which was also called Cuth. Nergal was worshiped until late in the time, with the most memorable images of him originating directly from Parthians. The Parthians controlled a vast multi-ethnic empire between 200 BC up to around 200 AD.

Nergal has been mentioned by the Bible as the patron deity for the city Cuth which is commonly called Cuthah. In the Bible, the Babylonian version of Nergal according to the Bible was Succoth-benoth. Talmudic scholars claim that Nergal was a reference to "dunghill the rooster" while the symbol for Nergal is the cockerel. Nergal is usually was associated by the image of the lion, which was his symbol. Nergal was said to be one of the children born to Ninlil as well as Enlil. His siblings included Ninurta as well as Nanna.

8. Was Sumerian mythology only confined to Mesopotamia?

Mesopotamia was an area that had a number of significant people, but also contained several people who would build Empires on their own through the years. It was home to the Sumerians along with The Akkadians comprised two most important groups that inhabited Mesopotamia however there were there were also other groups like the Assyrians, Hurrians, Chaldeans (Babylonians) and many others. The reason this picture so confusing is the fact that some of these older peoples, such as the Babylonians are likely to be the descendants of earlier peoples who existed living in the region. Thus, the development of Babylon was linked to the Amorite people, who weren't actually from Mesopotamia but rather from the Canaan/Phoenicia region. The Amorites do not appear to have completely replaced individuals who lived in Babylon as well as other cities in Sumer and Akkad So the more recent Babylonians are likely to be the result of intermarrying among Sumerians, Akkadians, Amorites, Assyrians, and whomever else was found in the area. The historians try to distinguish between Indo-Iranian and Indo-European populations in Mesopotamia however the debate is really a matter of semantics. Certain historians study Neanderthal remains from the region, and attempt to establish connections with that lineage.

Sumerian mythology was not limited to Mesopotamia. As we've observed, the idea of who was Mesopotamians and who were not was muddled by the waves of invasion and settlement. Be aware that Mesopotamia isn't just an agricultural region and straddles all continents, including Asia, Europe, and Africa. The Mesopotamian gods were easily able to flow out from Mesopotamia. Of course, the most obvious example of this was Inanna-Ishtar-Ashtoreth, but there were others as well.

9. What was the time line of Sumerian mythology and culture?

The history of Sumerian mythology and culture was extremely long and complicated. The first movements of Sumerian civilization began over 6000 years long ago. Sumerian civilization started as city-states with a single patron god (or several) would be worshipped. As Sumerian civilization grew more advanced and the polity of the city-state was replaced by empires - initially the Akkadian followed by later the Babylonian, Assyrian, and other gods - the gods began to be incorporated into the larger and bigger pantheons. Thus, the few gods of the cities eventually gave way to the pantheon of over 300 gods associated with the empires of the later Mesopotamia.

The civilization of this region Sumer could be believed to have continued to the time of Islam. It is possible to place a marker on the Islamization of the region as the conclusion of the mythology, since that was the point at which gods like Inanna were not worshipped. In fact, Mesopotamian gods had such powerful influence that they could be worshiped by Persia and sometimes are misinterpreted by some as Persian gods. It's tempting to make a comparison of the Sumerian mythology with other mythologies, such as the Greeks as well as the Norse of the northernmost part of Europe. When compared with these elaborate stories, Sumerian mythologies stand out in a unique and exhausting. The list of most important gods has evolved over time, something that cannot be said about Norse, the Greeks as well as Norse.

10. What was the reason that civilization began in Mesopotamia?

There are many reasons for why civilization was born in Mesopotamia. Actually, the primary academic task is to recognize that the majority of evidence available currently indicates Mesopotamia as the birthplace of civilization, a title that the region has enjoyed for a long time. Of course, we'll never know whether civilization started elsewhere, but the region is so submerged beneath oceans or cities that there are no traces. If you're a frequent viewer of cable TV or other channels, you might believe that civilization originated on another planet, and was brought to us by aliens.

But let's go back to Mesopotamia. Civilization started at Mesopotamia as a result of: (1) the fertile area was ideal for farming; (2) ample supplies of fresh water from two rivers enabled the large population to be sustained; (3) advanced agricultural technology allowed workers to be allocated to regions that were not part of agriculture. (4) Mesopotamia's central position probably allowed for the exchange of ideas which led to the growth of civilization, in contrast to what was happening in smaller areas.

11. What are the distinctive features that distinguish Sumerian religion?

Sumerian religion was distinctive in that a number of gods were anthropomorphic. Gods can be depicted using animals' bodies. They could be wearing the wings of animals connected the body. They could also have the feet of an animal. Sumerian faith was distinct due to the extent to the degree that syncretism saw gods from different religions mixed as the years progressed. This means the that, in many aspects Sumerian religion was ever-changing. Contrary to Greece where the relationship between gods was fairly fixed In Sumerian religion, gods' relations with each other could change. The name and persona of a god's wife could be changed, or a god could become the god of a god different from the one previously.

It is also fascinating to note that certain legends of Sumerian gods depict them as normal people who lived or were kings. They could be described as nomadic people who travel from one location to another. or as kings that visit cities, towns and other areas. This suggests that possibly certain Sumerian gods were both men and women who were immortalized by mythology. Another theory suggests that it was crucial for the Sumerians to think of their gods as similar to their own somehow.

12. Are the gods from Mesopotamia be considered to be the same as Egyptian, Greek, or Roman gods?

It's difficult to design an alignment system that aligns gods from Mesopotamia with gods from other mythologies, such as that of Greeks and the Egyptians. Mesopotamian gods were just different from gods of other pantheons, they were constantly in a change. The primary Sumerian god was not consistent through the Sumerian period. Therefore, we cannot say for instance that Enlil was the main Sumerian god and therefore should be compared to Zeus and Zeus, etc. Enlil was the chief god of the pantheon for a period of time however, in later times the most powerful gods included An (or the goddess Anu) Marduk, An (or Anu), Ashur, and even Inanna.

13. Did any gods of Mesopotamia have their place in other mythologies of great importance?

It has been suggested that some male Mesopotamian gods could have slipped to the gods and pantheons of different peoples which include the Phoenicians as well as the Greeks. It can be difficult to distinguish one god from one another, even in this context due to confusion over the names or titles. For instance, the term Ba'al, which translates to Lord is a reference to various Mesopotamian gods. One notable instance of a god that has been incorporated into various other pantheons is Inanna who was known under various names based on the person who worshipped her.

14. Ishtar is believed to be among the most well-known among the Sumerian and Mesopotamian gods as well as goddesses. What is the reason?

Ishtar appears to satisfy the need for a woman that was present throughout The Near East and other regions. Ishtar also known as, Inanna, was a goddess that had a strong sexual aspect. Inanna was not just an incarnation of sexual sex, love and passion, she was also an incarnation of war. There's a scene where Ishtar, also known as Inanna depicted with weapons to lead troops into battle. While doing so she may wear an outfit that shows off her legs or the beauty that her physique displays.

It is only natural that the Greeks could incorporate a version of Ishtar to their pantheon. Of course, it was Aphrodite who played an important role as the goddess of affection to the Greeks. Aphrodite was the protagonist in numerous important stories, including the Judgment of Paris as well as The Trojan War. It is interesting to note that Aphrodite in Greek mythology is usually not connected with conflict. This version of a goddess who was very sensual could have been higher than what the Greeks could bear. Whatever the reason Ishtar appears to have benefited not just from the importance of the position she had, but also because of the important role of the cities such as Babylon and other cities where she was extremely appreciated.

15. Sometimes, the gods and characters from mythology can prove to exist. Did any of the characters from Sumerian myths real?

This is a fascinating question. The widespread use of names between gods and the king lists suggest that one gods were actually living kings or that the kings got their names from the gods. Another possibility is that mythological tales were invented to celebrate the kings who controlled important cities. This may be the case in the legend of Atrahasis because Atrahasis is believed as a ruler of an important Sumerian city during the early time.

16. What is the reason it is important to know the background of Sumer in the course of doing research on Sumerian mythology?

One of the most fascinating aspect in Sumerian mythology is the fact that there was always more gods adding to the god pantheon. Additionally, the function of this god could shift. Knowing a bit of understanding of Sumerian history will help you comprehend the reasons why one god increased the importance of a particular period that spanned several centuries, and another god decreased. We've already discussed the way Enlil and Anu suffered a decrease in their importance as they lost much of their power to local gods like Ashur, Marduk, Amurru and many other gods. This is a great preamble to the question that follows.

17. What was the reason Sumerian goddesses and gods typically linked to cities?

Sumer and Mesopotamia was a region with big cities. They are better named city-states as in the beginning of the history of Mesopotamia the cities ruled over the large areas of land. The cities were governed by their own gods they worshipped. The gods of these cities were closely connected with the prosperity that the cities had. If a city performed well it was believed this was because of the help of gods. If the god was not successful to intervene, it could be read as if the god had abandoned the city, or that god had failed.

This kind of idea of civics was believed to be prevalent throughout the region of the Near East. In the Bible there are mentions of God being the God of Israel as being higher than any other god. This is a reflection of a belief that God represented the strength and vitality the people. In addition, since the people of the early Mesopotamia were organized into cities, this implied that gods favored cities. Cities constructed large, elaborate temples to worship their god. If a city was to establish an empire through the conquer of other cities, the god of that city would be a god in the pantheon, while also being associated with a specific place.

18. Are Anu the same as Zeus? If not, then who is?

Anu also known as An is a god of the sky. It's tempting to compare Anu with Zeus However, one has to be aware not to fall into a trap when it comes to this. Even though Anu was among the Seven Great Gods of Sumer (and even one of the three main gods), Enlil was frequently thought of as more central and significant in mythology in comparison to Anu. Because of this, comparing Anu with Zeus is not easy since Zeus was the king of the gods. Anu along with Enlil both had godfathers other than Zeus, and, therefore, as the All-Father or leader in The pantheon Enlil has more merits to the role of Anu. Anu may be thought of as a kind of Cronus as the leader of the Titans and the father of Zeus.

19. What is it that makes Sumerian mythology so unexplored when compared to other mythologies from other regions?

One reason to this is the complex nature of Sumerian gods. There were hundreds and their role in Sumerian life were changed throughout the centuries. Inanna (or Inanna) is known to many people today due to her name is often mentioned in class, but the majority of Sumerian gods are not known to the public. A further reason that explains the relative obscurity in Sumerian mythology is the fact that these gods are a long way away from the modern world, as well as in terms of time. They don't appear in Western films, TV shows or in books, so they appear as a bit odd and intriguing.

20. What effect did Ancient Sumerian civilization had on our lives in the present?

Many of the advances from the Sumerian period that we can take advantage of. Historical scholars hold the Sumerians responsible for the sixty second minute, the 60-minute hour as well as the year's division in twelve calendar months and the current practice of massive agriculture. In fact, there weren't cities prior to they were the Sumerians due to the fact that their Sumerian inhabitants who lived in Mesopotamia were the pioneers of civil living. The Sumerians were among the very first people to reside in cities, and were the first people to reside in the city-state as a unit of government. It's hard to imagine what the world would look like were it not because of the Sumerians and the many ways they brought to the ways people interact with the world around them.

21. What was the process by which Mesopotamian Gods and Goddesses expand across other regions?

Mesopotamia was a significant region due to a variety of reasons. It was also the source of many of techniques and practices that later have spread to other areas, Mesopotamia was also strategically located. It was one of the main attractions of the region, in both local kings and conquerors from outside. Mesopotamia separated the Western part of the Near East from Egypt and the Mediterranean Sea. This meant that people of Persia or Parthia

For instance, they had to traverse the region to get to their intended destinations. This is a part of the method by that Mesopotamian Gods and Goddesses were spread across different regions. Contact between strategically situated Mesopotamia with areas like Phoenicia and Persia enabled Mesopotamian beliefs to expand across these regions. The contact could have occurred through trade or been a result of the conquest. For instance, Mesopotamian gods likely spread to Persia following Babylon and the empire of Babylon was destroyed by Persia. However there is evidence that gods such as those of Phoenician Ashtoreth (who was based on the goddess Inanna/Ishtar) moved into Greece to be transformed into Aphrodite by trade.

22. What was hieros gamos , and why was it so important?

Hieros gamos , in fact an actual Greek word which refers to a sacred wedding. It was a wedding that was a marriage where the opposite of male and female joined to create cosmic life. This is another instance of the Sumerian concept of cosmic order, however it is also the basis for the connection between An and Ki in the birth of Enlil and later life. The story that tells of Enki and Ninhursag, to be told in the near future will explain the way Enki lives alongside his spouse in Dimun a paradise. Enki is the lord of Ab which means fresh water. However, it can may also mean male semen.

The idea of a sacred marriage is actually present in other cultures , besides Mesopotamia. In Hinduism there was a ceremony where girls were married to a temple. It was interpreted as a kind of marriage ceremony to gods that included dancing as well as other ceremonies. For the Greeks they believed that the marriage of Zeus as well as Hera was considered to be the most significant wedding ceremony, and it was re-enacted during ceremonies, specifically in the Greek island Samos in which the wedding was believed to have occurred. In Sumer the time was imperative that the kings make ceremonies of marriage solemn to the priestess Inanna to symbolize the union from which wellbeing and the life of the citizens in the city-state could spring.

23. What did you think of exactly the Atra-Hasis in Sumerian mythology?

Atrahasis also known as Atrahasis, or the Epic of Atrahasis, is the most comprehensive account about the Great Flood in Mesopotamian literature. The story was later adapted to be an element of the Epic of Gilgamesh though some of the characters' names were changed. It is believed that the Atrahasis (also known as Atra-Hasis) was written in the Akkadian period. It is important to remember it was it was written by the Akkadians are the tribe who lived in the immediate northwest of Sumerians properly. The Akkadian period, which started with the reign of King Sargon The Akkadians and Sumerians were united into one state, known by the name of The Akkadian Empire.

The Epic of Atrahasis was written in the 1800s BC. It was written using the Semitic Akkadian language upon clay tablets. The name signified that the the tablets contained a lot of wisdom. The tablets contained the Sumerian creation tale as well as the tale about the Great Flood. Atrahasis is not only the title of this work. The name is also listed as a name on the Sumerian King List which refers to a king from an Sumerian city-state, in this case, it is the Shuruppak city. Shuruppak. The king was a king in prehistoric time. The Atrahasis begins with events prior in the Deluge.

24. Who were the Seven Great Gods of Sumer?

The Seven Great Gods of Sumer were identified in the form of An, Enlil, Enki, Utu, Inanna (or Ishtar), Ninhursag, and Nanna. While sometimes used as a slang word to Annunaki, Igigi in the Epic of Atrahasis referred to the lesser gods that were the servants of Gods of the Seven Great Gods.

25. Who was the most famous Sumerian hero?

The most famous Sumerian hero was definitely Gilgamesh. Much like many Greek heroes, including Theseus, Gilgamesh was a real person who was the the king of the Sumerian city-state. Similar to Theseus, Sumerian acquired demigod status over time as the years went into the future. Gilgamesh was the head in the town of Uruk which was one of the largest cities in Sumer. Gilgamesh was the protagonist from The Epic of Gilgamesh, which was actually a sequence of poems. The poems were composed in various times and some are in better condition in preservation than other. The first of the poems were Gilgamesh, Enkidu, and the Netherworld. This poem is in which Gilgamesh sends his scurrying creatures in the vicinity of Inanna's huluppu. Following the demise of Enkidu, Gilgamesh learns of the situation in"the "Netherworld."

The Epic of Gilgamesh was composed of several poems that dealt with Gilgamesh's life. Gilgamesh. The epic's formal version was composed by a scribe known as Sin-leqiunninni in the year 1600 BC however, it was based upon epic poems composed earlier. Gilgamesh in the epic was a god who was in contact with Inanna (known as Ishtar at the time the epic was composed in the form of Ishtar). The actual Gilgamesh was an emperor who lived between 2900 BC between 2300 and 2900 BC. This puts him prior to the establishment of the Akkadian Empire by King Sargon. Even though there is no evidence of Gilgamesh's reign, one monument dating from the time of King Ishbi-Erra of Sumer is credited to Gilgamesh for the erection of the walls of Uruk. Uruk. Ishbi Erra was the king of Sumer around 1900 BC.

Chapter 3: Sumerian City States

While the Sumerian civilization was built upon agriculture, the Sumerian civilization was in its essence, an urban. This was a radical change from earlier societies, which typically comprised small, disconnected villages.

Sumerians were city-states and in the middle of each city, as mentioned previously was the temple of the god of their patron. The first temples constructed of clay bricks, later structures added different ornaments to the walls which made them more attractive.

Each city was thought as a part of the god of patrons. The temple, however, only held a portion of the land within the city, and it was rented out for the purpose of cultivation. The remainder part of it was owned by private individuals. They, along with the city's chief, "ensi," held all the power of the state and ruled on all major matters in concert.

The king was not a part of the beginning of Sumerian society. It was introduced later, as the discord between city-states became more violent. The King, or as it was known to the Sumerians call him "big man" was elevated to the position of supreme ruler, with his decisions being above the opinions of the common people. First kings were chosen from the assembly of cities in the time of crisis, to mobilize armies and plan city defenses.

In the course of time the system of the King's rule became one of the principal features in The Sumerian civilization. He ruled over massive armies made up of heavily armored and heavily armed infantry. All of these parts, together with well-organized leadership, strong military tactics, and a strong army, made a variety of Sumerian conquers possible.

Other than the elites and the soldiers Most of the Sumerian population consisted of fishermen, farmers and masons, cattle breeders and other craftsmen. While there were of course those powerful and rich citizens, the less powerful civilians owned homes and cattle. They sold their work on the market for sale trading them in exchange in exchange for other items or, often to purchase silver disks or rings that served as currency (shekels).

The facts regarding the internal structure of the Sumerian city-states do not agree with the writings of a few Oriental scholars who claimed the Sumerian society to be a theocracy entirely ruled by the Temple and its elite. Numerous documents dating from between 2,500 and 2,400 BC clear that the inhabitants of Sumer were free to possess the property and to sell it at any time. The stone tablets from Lagash records the purchase of property made by the king. It is clear evidence that the power of kings was limited, and even royalties could not seize the wealth they desired.

Though temples definitely owned significant parts of the land cities, the assertion that all property was held by the temple is not in line with the evidence found. Of of course the nobility held an important portion of the part of land however the majority of these estates were purchased from less wealthy citizens. It is evident that the Sumerian society wasn't perfect and, like all other societies in period, it favoured the wealthy elite, however it wasn't an open theocracy, in which priests (and the king) could make whatever they wanted.

The Division is part of the Society

Sumer's society Sumer was comprised of four main categories: nobility, common citizens clients, slaves, and nobility. Clients were members of the society who were in the service of the temple and nobility enjoyed the same status as those of serfs of feudal era.

There were three major types of customers. The ones who worked for the temple nobility were typically wealthy and included temple officials and skilled craftsmen. Another large number of patrons who worked for the temple, but with jobs that were less demanding. Then, there were nobles' clients, who were part of noble estates and received some percentage of their work, or receiving compensation for their service in a different manner.

Slavery was a significant institution in Sumerian society. The majority of slaves were prisoners of war, whether from another nation or Sumerians of other towns that were defeated by their armies in battle. There were also different ways that a person could be the slave.

Some free citizens were turned to slaves for punishment as punishment, and there were instances where parents, at the midst of crises and adversity, sold their children to slavery. Similar to other societies that accepted slavery as a legitimate institution, Sumerians saw their slaves as property of the commons and their fate was entirely dependent on their masters.

Based on what we have learned However, it is apparent that slave owners did not overuse their power to the extent that they did because it was their highest interests to ensure that their slaves were healthy and happy to enable them to perform better. The slaves also had certain legal rights, such as the right to purchase their freedom from slavery. Prices weren't set by law, but generally, buying slaves was generally less expensive than purchasing donkeys.

Incredibly, it appears that women were considered to be with respect in Sumerian society. They were permitted in business to possess property, and be witnesses. Although this was not typical for the time however, men were in an advantage.

The wedding was usually planned by the family and the wedding is considered legally binding when the groom's father was present with a wedding present. The men were free to divorce their wives with no reasons, and if the woman was unable to have children the husband was free to marry a second woman.

Law

It is evident from the information we know about the Sumerian civilizations that their lives were well-organized. Therefore, it's not a surprise that the written law was a key element in the life of the city-state.

The document, which dates from 2350 BC (the time of the Urukagina rule of

Lagash) could be one of the greatest documents of this kind. It is a comprehensive reform that brought an end to various violations committed by rulers and their entourage. The document also serves as an indication of the conflict of power between the palace and the temple which is perhaps the earliest instance of the battle among "the the church" in opposition to "the government."

Urukagina's report does not detail the circumstances that led to the abuses that prompted the necessity to make changes. We are aware that Lagash was severely damaged due to 200 years of bloody wars which had a limited success for a short periodof time, but eventually left the state in a very poor situation.

In the time of conquests, citizens of Lagash were stripped from their right and liberties. King s who were starving for glory needed soldiers to build their armies as well as food and other provisions to support the army. This could only be accomplished with force, by increasing taxes up to the limit and even by taking over the temple's property.

The populace resisted a bit during wartime however it transpired that after peace finally come the rulers were unwilling to let go of their new streams of money. They maintained their rule with a ferocious hand and severely punished those who did not pay taxes or who dared to speak against the established. Even those who passed away weren't freed of the obligations they incurred, and their families were immediately released of their possessions to pay off the dues.

These practices did no good luck in the city of Lagash. The ruling elite was making fortunes while the rest of the population was forced to live in living in poverty. In the works of a modern scholar, the artisans were frequently placed in a position to begging for food and slaves were treated as animals, while the wealthy kept growing their fortunes. People who were less fortunate were compelled to sell their homes and other assets in exchange for a small amount of money and they had no protection who could protect their interests.

The newly-elected Urukagina, the king of Lagash, was determined to put an end to this. He was a religious, god-fearing person, who was aware of the plights the people of Lagash faced, and decided to say "enough."

He enacted new laws which stopped the confiscation of property. He ended payment of ensis and viziers after a man divorced his wife. The king also ended the scavenging practices of preying on the families of dead by severely restricting what tax collectors and other officials could claim upon death.

Urukagina made sure that no one had to beg for food any longer. He set up food rations for the guilds of craftsmen as well as other artisans, workers, and apprentices. He enacted laws to stop wealthy people from twisting the hands of poor by allowing them to sell their properties at a lower price than the actual value and released everyone who was unfairly detained for not paying taxes. He also signed a contract with the god of patrons Ningirsu to ensure that any man with power cannot commit unfairness against orphans or widows.

Another source of Sumerian written laws is Ur-Nammu, a code written as the founding document of Ur, the Third Dynasty of Ur. The code dates back to 2050 BC which was close to the conclusion in the Sumerian period. Even the fact that these finds are of a an older date with respect to the Sumerian civilization, it's possible to conclude that they are based on the customs and laws by the people who lived during the time before the text.

When it comes to the court system, it appears that courts were typically comprised from three to four judges. It was not their primary job, since they came from different walks of life, including temple officials, city elders, merchants, scribes, etc. There is however evidence that suggests there was a royal court located in Nippur where seven judges of the royal court was in charge.

In the course of trials, testimony were made under an oath. Some were presented by witnesses, and at other times, by public officials or experts. Once the decision was reached it was only put into effect after the parties who were deemed by the court swore in the temple. This proved to be the final evidence of their claim.

Architecture of the city of Sumerian City

Although we can be fairly certain we can say that Sumerian city-states were massive and populated with a lot of people, the precise numbers can be difficult to establish. There is no evidence of any census that was conducted in the time period and makes estimating difficult.

The population estimate for Lagash was about 100,000. Its city, Ur which was the capital city of Sumer in the year 2000 BC was home to a estimated population of around 360,000. The number of people who lived there, as stated in the year 2000 by C. L. Woolley may be exaggerated, however it is certain that the population of the city was around the 200,000th soul.

Based on the findings by Woolley as well as other scholars, besides the temple's area, Sumerian cities were not very attractive cities. The roads were small and unpaved, and houses both small and large were clustered together without specific arrangement. It is evident there was no plan for the Sumerian town was never planned however, it was formed by bringing a variety of villages and functionally linking them, with no concern for what is refer to as "urban development."

The Sumerian homes were for the most part, single-story houses constructed of the mud bricks. The wealthier people could have two-story homes with a dozen rooms. These buildings were typically whitewashed and plastered.

The furnishings inside comprised the tables that were low, chairs and beds made of wooden frames. The walls and floors were covered in woolen hangings and skin rug. It was not unusual for a mausoleum of a family to be hidden beneath the house.

Knowledge and Science

Sumerian cities relied on craftsmen and artisans. They were not awe-inspiring in any theoretical field as in our knowledge. Their definition of the world's natural phenomena was very basic. Even astronomy that was popularized in Babylon was largely unexplored. We can speculate that the Sumerians were aware of the celestial bodies in some degree but there is no evidence to prove this claim.

There were two distinct seasons for the calendar The"emesh" or summer ("emesh") was in March or February, while winter ("enten") began in February or March. ("enten")"enten") was in September or October. In the case of New Year, it was celebrated in September or October. New Year was most likely observed in April or May.

They were lunar in nature, beginning with the evening of the new moon. It lasted between 29 and 30 days. The names of the months are derived from the activities of agriculture or celebrations to honor certain gods.

The day was split into two 12 hour time periods. The day officially began with sunset. The night was divided into three separate watches that ran 4 hours each. The water clock was used to track the time. They may have employed the shadow clock too.

In terms of medicine, there are two tablets that date back to that of the Sumerian period. One tablet does not give much detail, since it is only one prescription. The other has fifteen prescriptions. It was written in the third period of the 3rd millennium BC.

The prescriptions of 15 can be divided into three categories based on the way that the medications were applied. In the first category the prescriptions are distributed in eight groups that can be used as poultices. The second group includes three prescriptions that contain medication that are intended for use internally. In the third group, there are drugs for which the procedure of use isn't clear. They are supposed for placement (arranged) on the feet and hands of the person who is sick however the reason for why this location was recommended is not clear.

The Sumerian doctors discovered the ingredients they needed to create their medicine from nature. They utilized minerals such as salt as well as river bitumen as well as animal parts such as milk, turtle shells and wool. But, the herbs were most vital ingredient in the creation of medicine. Plants such as figs, pears as well as mustard and pine played an important role in Sumerian medicine.

It is interesting to note that the discovered medical texts don't contain any mention of magic or religion. These are quite common in similar texts of older civilizations, so the fact that there's no references to magic or religion in Sumerian texts is a bit of a surprise. The doctors of the ancient Sumer appeared to be to be, extremely sensible.

Arts

The Sumerians are known for their talents in the art of sculpture. Their style of expression was abstract. The statues of temples are centered on displaying emotion and energy instead of the skill of the artist. The sculptures found offer valuable information about Sumerian fashion of dressing and the general style of their appearance.

Men either had beards that were long or well-groomed. They wore skirts and jackets with cloaks. A shawl was slung on the left shoulder while the right arm was left free. Women wore dresses similar to long shawls. They covered the entire body from head to foot. The right shoulder was left unattended. The hair was braided into a long thick pigtail that was wrapped around their head.

Music was also a major part of the culture of an Sumerian city. Within the town of Ur the harps and lyres were discovered. Drums and tambourines were also frequently utilized. Poetry and singing were popular too, with themes typically centered around the worship of their gods and kings.

One of the most significant achievements to one of the most significant contributions made by Sumerian civilisation is its seal of the cylinder. This was an engraving stone and the meaning behind the engravings became apparent after it was placed onto a tablet of clay, or sealing. Their craftsmen developed exquisite and intricate designs to use to seal their seals. The invention is later replicated by other civilizations like the ones that of Greece, Egypt, and Cyprus.

Farming

We have mentioned many times, agriculture was the core of the Sumerian city-state. It's not surprising that they spent much of their time finding ways and methods to streamline agricultural operations and improve the yield of their crops.

In reality, an entire "farming Almanac" was found to contain guidelines for everyday farming. The text is the text of 107 lines. Its translation proved difficult, in particular due to the numerous technical terms employed.

The manual covers everything starting with the pre-planting of the field and equipment to the harvesting and cleaning. Farmers are advised to first thoroughly plough the ground prior to planting. Following planting, the land must be leveled and cleared so that the seeds can sprout more easily.

The next step is to offer prayers at the Goddess of vermin that eats the crops. Sumerian doctors were possibly extremely rational, however common farmers were convinced that their only chance to achieve success in their work was to ask gods to bestow their blessings on their crops and protect them.

The guide will then explain the method of watering as well as the ideal time to harvest. After harvesting, it's time to thresh and lastly, winnowing to sort the chaff from the grain.

The guide is detailed and comprehensively goes through every step in the context of this guide, its significance is because the Sumerian civilization was sophisticated enough to comprehend and record all of these methods. This was among the many, if not the primary factors that led to their long-lasting and incredible advancement.

We'd be remiss not to note that the most popular drinks of Sumerians included beer. Numerous texts claim beer as a drink that enthralls the in the people of both gods and mortals. The brewing methods they used aren't entirely clear, but we know there was a goddess who was responsible for the preparation of beer. Namely, her name was Ninkasi"Ninkasi" - "the lady who filled your mouth."

Chapter 6: Contributions

Two of the major Sumerian contributions to the subsequent civilizations was the creation of cuneiform writing as well as the system of education that was the direct result of literacy. Writing and learning started in Sumer and, from there, were spread throughout the world.

The development in the area of education was not rapid but it was a steady one. In the middle three millennia BC several schools were operating throughout Sumer. The students in these schools were as well taught to write. The tablets found in the vicinity of the city Shuruppak which dates back to around 2500 BC were the first textbooks used in schools which included gods, animals and a variety of terms and phrases.

In the second half in the 3rd millennium the Sumerian education system began to flourish. This is evident from the large number of clay tablets excavated to this time. There was a substantial increase in the number of scribes trained for specific categories, like administration and state affairs.

But the tablets do not provide information on the way the school system actually functioned. To discover this it is necessary to search for writings from 2000 and 1500 BC. A few tablets from this time were discovered, containing various writing exercises. The exercises range from easy attempt for beginners, to the elaborate work of more advanced students.

A number of essays that describe the methods of teaching and strategies used in the schools of the ancient Sumer are also available These works can reveal a lot about the method of operation and the objectives of the educational system.

Edduba is the home of tablets

Sumerian schools were known as "edduba," which translates to "tablet home." Their primary goal was to produce skilled professionals to carry out many official duties which were mostly for the palace and temple. With the development of educational system, they have also become a source of education for the Sumerian schools have become centres of culture for the state.

Sumerian scholars who spent their time studying various sciences they learned about theology as well as botany, geography along with creative writing. The teachers and students were the ones to translate the old documents, and then wrote their own. Similar to the present, many Sumerian teachers dedicated their lives entirely to research and teaching.

The schooling as it was wasn't compulsory, and was generally reserved for the most wealthy members of society. A list compiled by Nikolaus Schneider, who was around 2000 BC includes the names of about 500 Scribes. All were descendants of wealthy citizens having important posts, such as governors naval officers, governors and sea captains and supervisors, for instance. It's also fascinating to observe there is only one name of a female is listed on the list, suggesting the fact that Sumerian education was mostly a man-centric affair.

The Sumerian educational system evolved primarily because of the need. They created a system to teach their students to write in the Sumerian language. The language was divided into several categories of related terms and phrases, which students were required to learn by their hearts. They would then learn ways to spell these terms until they were proficient in it.

In addition to those lists which had the names of cities, animals minerals, cities and so on. Additionally, there were several tablets that held mathematical knowledge. For the study of grammar and linguistics the subjects were examined in depth. In reality what is most likely the oldest dictionary that has been discovered by mankind dates to the close period of Sumerian period.

When the Akkadians took on Sumer in the year 900, they displayed an intense curiosity about their literature as well as their own language. As the language disappeared after the war and they had to create dictionaries in order to study their writings.

The bulk of the work performed during the Sumerian schools was transcription and copying of old texts. There were hundreds of these texts, mostly composed of a poetic variety. We've already discussed the works of these authors, such as epics and myths that comprised the bulk in the Sumerian literary works.

As we can tell we know, a typical day for students at Sumerian school would look like this. He would begin his study on his tablet that he made one day prior and begin working on a tablet given to him to him by his teacher. The ability to remember things in a heart-beat played a significant role in the Sumerian education system.

The beginning students would begin with basic exercises. Once they'd learned the basics of syllables, they moved onto a detailed sign list that contained more than 800 entries. Following signs, were important words that consisted from two signs or even more. These lists included the names of organs in humans animals, bird parts as well as stars.

Once a student had become familiar in the intricate Sumerian dictionary, they would continue to work on writing by copying sentences from simple products. Another crucial aspect of the process of training was the ability to write models contracts, since they were crucial to the economy of Sumer. Along with writing, students studied basic mathematics, particularly measurements for length, weight capacity, weight, etc.

The discipline at Sumerian schools was extremely rigorous. The cane was likely to be one of the most important instruments for discipline. Education was, therefore very difficult, since students were spending a lot of time in the classroom.

As of today, a number of schools that could be from ancient Mesopotamia have been discovered. One of them is within the town of Nippur while the other located in Ur and the third in Ur. There was nothing to differentiate these structures from regular houses, apart from the tablets found there. But, more recent findings in Nippur have discovered classroom-like areas with benches made from baked brick.

"Schoolday," the essay "Schoolday" is among the best preserved documents that explains what a typical day was like within the Sumerian classroom. It was written around 2000 BC. There are certain striking similarities between students of the ancient times and the students of today. Much like the students of today students of the past, a student from the past of Sumer was also scared to miss school, and was worried about the consequences.

If a student is found to be in trouble during class, he's punished at the direction of his instructor. Teachers, on the other hand the sums up to their earnings was similar to that of modern teachers. To make money to live they Sumerian teachers might find a way to receive a gift from their parents.

Chapter 7: Sumerian Literature

For many ancient civilizations, the primary sources of information about them stem from archeological finds that comprise fragments of buildings as well as their weapons, jewellery and pots, as well as other items. It is our responsibility to draw decisions and develop the concepts about their beliefs and lives from these evidences by putting together their stories as a huge puzzle comprising many different pieces.

The Sumerians However, this isn't the case. While there are many archeological evidences of the kinds mentioned above, explorations have also revealed a variety of written records made of clay that describe the history of Sumer in the form of actual sentences. A majority the documents administrative or economic nature and reveal a few interesting facts. However, there are about five thousand tablets that include various literary works.

A few tablets are stuffed with hundreds of pages of text, while others are just small fragments comprising a couple of dozen words that are often damaged and unfinished. The literary fragments which have been put together somewhat or in all their parts show us a very high degree of cultural and spiritual development.

The Sumerian writings are among the oldest of the literary works that have been discovered by mankind. As of today it is believed that nothing more ancient has been discovered in the past, and it is likely that anything more ancient is likely to be discovered in the near future. Translating and putting together their writings isn't an easy job however it is among the most crucial aspects to understand the evolution of civilization and not just the Sumerians however, but also all human civilizations which was the predecessor to those of the early peoples from Mesopotamia were.

Fortunately for modern travelers and explorers, the Sumerian writers were in the habit of making multiple duplicates of the identical tablet. Therefore, even if one tablet found damaged, what's missing can be identified from another identical tablet that was found in the same or a different place.

It is possible to conclude that the Sumerians began writing in 2500 BC. In this time there is a clay-based cylinder with an ancient myth of Enlil, the god of the gods, and Ninhursag his wife. The myth also makes reference to other Sumerian gods, such as Enki or Inanna. The cylinder may be too damaged to be able to discern the specific plot, design elements are similar to the ones found in later writings.

From the collection of discovered tablets that were written over decades, it's clear that Sumerian literature was constantly evolving. The first literature was studied and removed, and the majority of the works we are currently reading have come into our hands in modified version.

Even though Sumerian cities were built around temples, and that their gods played a significant part in daily life however, their literature was not exclusively of a religious nature. Priests certainly were involved in the creation of hymns and laments however, the epics of heroic proportions such as those on Lugablanda and Gilgamesh were rarely performed in temples.

Minstrel (or "nar) (or "nar") was the principal character of the Sumerian writing process. They probably were students from "edubba" (Sumerian schools of scribal writing). These were the sole locations where literature was kept, and they also had libraries that were large. The books from these libraries were used to teach, but also for gatherings with the public and temple readings, among other things.

The poetry was the principal method of expression used by the Sumerians. While they didn't use rhyme and meter the other poetic tools are used in the writings that their poetry writers. Similes, metaphors and other strategies were employed to produce vivid and captivating images. In terms of story, it appears it was not among the primary concerns, since the narratives tend to be different and there's no sense of progress toward the conclusion. The characters are typically characters, with broader traits and their uniqueness is seldom emphasized.

Myths

The list of widely rediscovered Sumerian myths can be a lengthy one. Some of them include "The The Creation of the Pickax,"" "Enki And Nimmah, The Creation of Man," and "Inanna's Descent to the Nether World." Other myths discovered are "Inanna as well as Bilulu," "The Marriage of Dumuzi and Inanna," "The Death of Dumuzi," and several others.

The myth of "Enki as well as the World Order" is perhaps one of the best examples of the Sumerian approach to writing mythologically. With 460 lines total, it opens with a hymn that praises the god Enki as the one who watches the universe. Then, the text goes on to speak of other gods in his voice. Enki himself.

In the next paragraphs, the poet discusses numerous rituals carried out by the priests of the shrine of Enki. Many of the lines from this chapter have been damaged beyond restoration making it difficult to comprehend the significance of these sections. When the text is finished it describes Enki aboard his boat with sea creatures giving respect and the wealth is recognized throughout the world.

He continues to decide the duties of the gods and goddesses, assigning to each of them their responsibilities (their "me"). Enki continues to visit various cities, such as Ur and Meluhha to bestow his blessings on the land and creatures. Cities like Marhashi and Elam which aren't favorable to Enki are destroyed and their riches purged.

In the next stage, in the following steps, God will fill Tigris with water that is fresh and creates the fish and invokes the rain that gives life in addition to other things. He also assigns various Gods and Goddesses oversee these new creations , and make sure that everything is right. He is responsible for the requirements of the farmer, giving them the right tools and the information needed to construct the homes. Enki determines the boundaries between cities and states, and grants God Ur the right to govern the universe.

In this moment in the myth In this scene, the goddess Inanna is unhappy because Enki didn't give her any particular duties to fulfill. She believes she was unfairly treated and is demanding that this injustice be corrected. Enki is trying to rationalize with her by pointing out that she is able to perform numerous important tasks and abilities, including the ability to demolish her own "indestructible."

In this moment, we have reached the conclusion of the salvaged portion of the legend. There are just some lines missing as well as from similar texts, we could assume that the story closes with a short anthem in honor of Enki.

Epics

Moving away from myths and fables, we come to epics as another way of expressing these ancient civilisations. Unfortunately, we don't have any epics from epics from the Sumerian epics as they were originally written. They were typically written in the time in which writing was not yet a thing and the majority of these epics of the early period were written about a hundred years after the period of great courage when they were first developed.

The Sumerian epics are mostly individual stories, each confined to one episode. There is a clear absence of enthusiasm in the writers to link these stories into a bigger and connected piece. In the myths heroes are general types instead of individuals, and they are a symbol of superior values, with minimal, if any personal growth. In contrast to the epics of later times of Indo-European countries mortal women do not have a significant role to play when it comes to Sumerian writings. However it is quite probable that this epic in its form, came in Sumer and was later adopted by other civilizations, and then adapted over time.

In all there are nine Sumerian epics discovered up to now. Four of them are centered around the characters Enmerkar and Lugalbanda, whereas the remaining five feature the well-known Gilgamesh as the central character. Three of these epics were preserved nearly all of them: "Gilgamesh and the Land of the Living," "Gilgamesh and Agga of Kish," and "Gilgamesh, Enkidu, and the Nether World."

The epic "Gilgamesh and Agga of Kish," albeit very small, is quite fascinating because it doesn't contain any reference to mythology or gods. It is a strictly human story and outlines some of the first struggles among those Sumerian cities. According to a legend Kish was the city that Kish was granted its "kingship" from gods following the massive Flood. However, the power of Erech continued to grow and eventually began to threaten to take over the throne of Kish. To stop the possibility of this happening, the ruler Agga, the ruler of Kish, Agga, sent an ultimatum to Gilgamesh the head of Erech and Erech: submit to us or face consequences.

As a true hero Gilgamesh did not seem to be enthusiastic about the thought of losing without a fight. When he received the ultimatum Gilgamesh calls the city council and asks whether they would support his fight against Kish. The senators don't share his enthusiasm, and are determined on surrendering and living their lives peacefully.

Gilgamesh dissatisfied by his attitude, gathers young men from Erech and pleads with the men to fight on his side. Contrary to the city's elders, young men back Gilgamesh and declare victory for independence.

After just two hours, Agga attacks Erech and is able to defeat its
army. Gilgamesh is able to get one of his warriors to speak to Agga however, Agga is captured, beat and humiliated.

In despair of a way out, Gilgamesh himself climbs the wall to confront Agga and Agga face-to-face. After the Kish ruler notices his courage and agrees to end the battle and leave Erech alone. Erech to its own. The last lines of the epic continue to be a celebration of Gilgamesh as the city's savior.

The second epic in the collection, "Gilgamesh and the Land of Living," tells the story of the fear of death. The Lord Gilgamesh is constantly stricken by thoughts of death while he watches the dying of men in Erech. This makes him conscious that he is mortal. He is awakened by the idea that he as well, will die the same way as everybody else.

Determined to establish his name known before death comes knocking on his doorstep, Gilgamesh embarks on the journey to the Land of the Living, hoping to bring its famous Cedars to Erech. As per guidance from the loyal assistant

Enkidu the first step is to make an offer to the god Utu who is the god over the Land of the Living. While initially skeptical, Utu promises to help Gilgamesh in his mission and Gilgamesh with his fifty companions begins his journey.

After a long journey, Gilgamesh finally finds "the cedar of his heart." He cuts it down using his axe, however, this act awakens Huwawa one of Huwawa's protectors in the Land. Huwawa slams the hero into an eerie sleep, and his companions are able to get him back an enormous amount of work.

Gilgamesh is deeply upset over the news, and vows to never return to Erech before he is able to kill Huwawa. Despite Enkidu's insistance to return, Gilgamesh is steadfast in his resolve to take on the fierce beast and keep his vow.

As they are aware that the leader of their group will not be dissuaded, they decide to join Gilgamesh to complete this risky task. Gilgamesh cut through the trees that block Huwawa's entrance into the inner chamber, and is brought confronted by the monster. He is able to trap him using his nose ring and rope and the monster begins pleads with Gilgamesh to give him his life. The hero is determined on showing Huwawa mercy However, Enkidu warns him to oppose. The monster scolds Enkidu and Enkidu reacts by cutting off his neck.

The epic concludes in a surprising manner. Gilgamesh and Enkidu take Huwawa's head that was cut off to God Enlil as a gift and hope for a reward from God. However, Enlil curses them both to walk across plains and mountains for the rest of their lives.

In the final chapter "Gilgamesh, Enkidu, and the Nether World," our hero has a variety of anti-qualities and qualities and vice versa, all within the same persona. He is the knight and the warrior, an astrologer and a depressing whiner. Enkidu is his faithful companion and servant, but does not honor his master at the crucial time that leads to his (Enkidu's) death.

The epic begins with a description of the divine actions of creation and Enki's struggle with the nether realm. The outcome of the conflict is not revealed while the writer continues to the tale of Gilgamesh.

In the past the willow tree was placed on the bank of Euphrates. In the past, South Wind picked up the tree and carried it to the river. Innana was awestruck and decided to bring it back to Erech, the city. Erech and put it in her garden. She was planning to build the throne, or a couch out of it when it was big enough.

As time went on, it was impossible to find any branches nor leaves in the trees. This was due to a snake that built a nest near the bottom. Then, at the top the Imdgud bird positioned its young. And in the middle the vampire Lilith was living in her home.

Innana was devastated by this and first appealed God Utu to assist her. In the end, when the sun god was unable to help and she decided to turn to Gilgamesh. Always up for a challenge and a challenge, the hero snatched his armor and an axe and went on to end the snake's life. After seeing this, the two others fled, and Gilgamesh chopped down the tree , and then gave the tree to Inanna to use according to her wishes.

To show her thanks, Inanna created a drum and a drumstick , and gave the two to Gilgamesh. But the lord of Erech employed these tools to oppress his people through appointing young men to fight for him at any time he wanted. Many young ladies call out to gods and in retribution the two objects fell into the "great home."

Because Gilgamesh did not succeed in retrieving the drum Enkidu was able to help. He wanted to go to the netherworld to retrieve the items that were lost. In spite of his master's clear instructions regarding what he should and should not be doing, Enkidu failed to follow these instructions and was eventually confined to the dark netherworld.

In a state of shock over what happened to his faithful friend, Gilgamesh first pleaded to Enlil for assistance However, the supreme God did not seem willing to help him. He then took his plea to Enki then the god of wisdom was determined to assist.

Enki instructed Utu to make a door between the two realms, and, through this passageway Enkidu's spirit came back to earth. Gilgamesh is unsure of the spirit of his friend (as is all the latter is or will be following his trip to the nether realm) about the way that dead are treated in the nether world. The epic is brought to an abrupt conclusion.

Hymns, lamentsations, and songs of praise

Beyond epics and myths the hymns played an important part in Sumerian literature. Many songs from this period has been found, with different lengths and in length. This is just a tiny portion of the amount of hymns composed.

These songs can be classified into four categories depending on the person or thing they honor Gods, kings or temples. The particular kind of hymns is interspersed prayers that include the worship of gods, and prayers for kings.

In the divine hymns, the poet may addresses a god, or praises his god(dess) for all the good things they've done. A few of the most important hymns of this type are the hymn to Enlil

Chapter 8: The Sumerian Motivation and System Of Values

There are many studies that describe the Sumerian economic, political and religious systems but there are only a few that provide a more thorough study of mental aspects that shaped their society. What were the motivations and motivations that drove the people to act? We know that devotion and religion played an significant roles in their lives. But the question is what do these convictions and convictions manifest into actions?

Similar to modern-day people like us, like modern people, Sumerians were also driven by three main emotions: hate, love and fear. It is believed that the Sumerian term for love can be translated literally as "to determine the size of earth." They also had the different kinds of love, including sensual love as well as affection among family members, between friends, and obviously, love between gods, kings and ordinary people.

In the case of marriage, we've said that it was primarily an practical arrangement. However, it wasn't without romantic gestures as shown by a variety of uncovered poems about courtships before marriage.

These poems may suggest that some marriages weren't functional and devoid of romantic sentiments. At times, the marriages were driven by passion and love however, the wedding as an institution was generally viewed as a serious issue and, in some cases even an obligation. When a couple got married regardless of their previous sentiments, they had to live a fairly dull life that often caused the gradual extinction of romantic feelings that were initially romantic.

No matter what, the family was of the highest importance to the Sumerian society. Families were close and being held together with reverence and love. There are many passages that support this belief, such as the saying: "... the wife is the future of man while the son is man's refuge; and the daughter is human's salvation ..."

It is clear from the quote above that the bond with children's parents significant one. Parents take care of their children, and as a result children were expected to be respectful of their parents. The most intimate relationship between fathers and son is one that is filled with love and understanding. The evidence supports this in a variety of articles and in the myths.

Family values, including respect, laws and understanding are frequently portrayed as stereotypes in Sumerian myths. Similar to the connection between parents and children, the bond between a sister and a brother was also one of strength. In certain instances the brother assumes the role of the father. This is evident in the story of Inanna who calls the brother Utu to assist her in getting rid of the snake which is encroaching the sacred tree of Erech.

While friendship was not thought of in the same way as family bonds but it was an important aspect of Sumerian culture. The most compelling evidence of this is the friendship that existed between Gilgamesh and his loyal servant and close friend Enkidu. Enkidu was willing to do anything to make his master content, which was far more than his position demanded from him. However as we've seen this, it ultimately cost him his life.

In the case of the relation between gods and humans it is obvious that people from Sumer considered themselves the slaves of their gods. But, a deeply embedded belief in the personal God suggests that Sumerians have a relationship with God. is that between parents and their children. The God they regarded as their personal God was someone they could always turn to in all circumstances regardless of the difficulties they faced They were always willing to listen to and seek help from the gods of heaven.

Chapter 9: The Importance of Sumerian Heroes and Rulers

The book is not complete without mention of the names and achievements of at least a few of the most notable historical figures of the early Sumer. As with all civilizations, Sumerians had their leaders who played key role in major conflicts as well as the internal accomplishments of the state. Names of the leaders and heroes are intricately linked to the story of Sumer as in general.

As we've stated in Chapter 5, there aren't any historical documents that were left by the Sumerian Scribes. In the light in the Sumerian worldview was not something their writers attempted to document in a manner as was observed by historians of the other civilizations. Everything that happened throughout the world was planned by the gods in the context of their mysterious and incomprehensible plans for the human race.

The closest thing we can find to the texts of the time of the ancient Sumer are the manuscripts that document efforts of kings and cities-state leaders (ensi's) on the building and embellishing temples. The recordings were not driven by historicalevents, but due to religious reasons, since priests and scribes sought to leave proof of their devotion and fidelity to their ancestors to follow.

Stone tablets and clay were not the only materials that were used by the first "historians." They wrote down their observations on stones, bricks statues and bowls as well as statues plaques, bowls, and everything else that could accept written cuneiform. The early texts are the sole source of Sumerian history in the early centuries following they came up with writing.

Another significant group of documents that can be used as an historical resource are various administrative and economic texts that date back between 2500 BC and onwards. For us, it is a blessing that Sumerian Scribes had an ingenious method to date their documents as well as particular events, making it possible to locate them under the reigns of specific rulers.

A key element of this scheme for dating is the known as the "King List." It lists details of major Sumerian rulers, along with the details of how long they reigned. However, historically speaking this list isn't very precise, since the writer identified the dynasties in terms of how they were in strict succession. In the majority of cases, the dynasties of these were usually contemporaneous. In addition, when it comes to the duration of specific reigns, some rulers are given an excessive amount of time. As a result, the list is spread over the time span that stretches over 250 years. In spite of these errors The list, when employed correctly, can be an extremely valuable resource to establish an historical timeframe.

The other aspect that is crucial to research the Sumerian historical record is what might be called "royal correspondence". Two letters were exchanged between certain state officials and rulers exchanged throughout the course of time. There are a few of these letters dating back to the 24th century BC. However, historically speaking the most significant of these letters are from the period that was the Third Dynasty of Ur. In these letters, we will find the motivations and explanations of the most important events of the time period.

As with other documents the letters were not found in their original forms, however, they are copies of originals made by students and teachers of different Sumerian schools.

Though they're the best examples of creative writing, Sumerian ethics are also an important source for research into the past. Nine epics that have been preserved all of them include a great deal of details about significant people and historical events.

The epic "Gilgamesh and Agga of Kish" is of major significance for understanding the political institutions of Sumer. It's not just a glimpse into the ongoing conflicts between Sumerian city-states but also lets us know the significance of decisions taken in Sumer. The congress or assembly formed to decide by Gilgamesh to decide whether there would be war demonstrates the fact that Sumerian rulers, though strong and well-respected but were unable to make crucial decisions important importance independently. They required approval and backing of the city's elders.

Lamentations as well as hymns, myths and lamentations can also give us historical facts. Lamentations, which typically contain descriptions of destruction to Sumerian cities, can provide valuable information about historical events. For instance, the oldest known lamentation, written upon a stone tablet is about the devastation from the city Lagash with some background information. The later lamentations, however, are usually limited to descriptions of horrific incidents, and provide very little actual details.

Myths, even though they are not historically in the sense that they are, usually offer a few unintentional, but nevertheless valuable insights. The events described in these myths may contain reference to actual events and people who played a part in the evolution of Sumerian civilization.

The multitude of sources in conjunction with the fact that we do not have no evidence of the historical period that spans the early two millennia of Sumer makes it very difficult for scholars to construct a complete background of the ancient civilization. It is difficult to distinguish the real from the imaginary, and reality from fiction is often an unattainable task.

We know for certain is that Sumerians were not the only people to reside in the regions of Mesopotamia. While there aren't any archaeological evidence that has been discovered prior to the Sumerian civilization , we can draw this conclusion through the linguistic evidence. For instance, the names that were originally used of the river Euphrates as well as Tigris, "idilgat" and "buranun" aren't Sumerian terms. This is also true for several significant Sumerian cities. We can therefore conclusively say that these locations were named by different people who resided in the region prior to when the Sumerians.

After this lengthy introduction, the first ruler from the Sumerian state we have an account of in writing was Etana from Kish. It is believed that he was ruled by Etana of Kish during the 3rd millennium. In the above King List the King List, he is described as the person who "stabilized all the land." King Etana was certainly an prominent and highly acclaimed persona from his Sumerian civilization. A different listing on the King List describes him as "the person who went into heaven." He was a god-fearing and religious leader, but in spite of all that, he couldn't not have children.

Due to this curse, Etana was determined to find his "plant for birth" believing that it would solve his issues. The plant, however, was in heaven and was far from mortals' reach. The King eventually enlisted the assistance of an eagle that could reach the sky and according to legends the King found the gods a new home.

Following Etana The King List mentions seven kings of whom we have very little to no information. Then there is the king Enmebaraggessi. His rule is at a minimum described in Sumerian writings. He was the ruler of the city of Kish and according to a few documents, he might have attempted to increase his influence over several of Sumerian city-states.

The son of Enmebaraggessi Enmerkar succeeded to the throne and was one of the most well-known people from the Sumerian civilization. Based on the information found in the King's List

Enmerkar was the one who built Erech as a city Erech and led the army against Aratta. One of his faithful companions during his battles were the hero Lugalbanda whom is mentioned in a variety of Sumerian epics. Lugalbanda was the first to be crowned following Enmerkar and, given his appearance in epics, it is likely that he would be an impressive ruler.

At this point it is clear that the legend and actuality are intricately interwoven with Sumerian historical records. The names of their kings are those of the deities as well as mythical heroes. The person who was elevated to the throne following Lugalbanda was King Dumuzi who was a key participant in the previously mentioned ritual of "holy wedding."

Following Dumuzi, Gilgamesh became the King. The amount of epics detailing Gilgamesh's adventures as well as the hero Gilgamesh clearly shows that his contribution to the evolution of Sumerian society was a significant one. Gilgamesh became a symbol of an adventurous and courageous man whose desire for fame and immortality never ceases to force him to challenge the limits. In actuality, the narratives of his adventures within The Sumerian epics have baffled historians throughout many centuries. The extent of their repercussions is so great that scholars are left wondering whether he actually was an actual person or the product of imagination.

Mesannepadda, the King
Mesannepadda was the first ruler of the First Dynasty of Ur and He conquered Nippur, the capital city. Nippur in order to take it from Agga who was the final leader of the First Dynasty of Kish. But, as per available evidence Mesannepadda seemed to be an elderly man and was later succeeding by his son Meskiagnunna. He was ultimately defeated by Gilgamesh who, at the time he was defeated, was an old man.

The complicated nature of events and difficulty in determining exact times of rulers and kings is result of the lack of or insufficient historical documents. It is apparent that a lot of these rulers lived in similar periods, and their spheres of influence led to conflict.

These wars significantly weakened the Sumerian state until the kingship was transferred to the Awan kingdom. Awan following Awan's First Dynasty of Ur. It is not clear the exact date and time Sumer was in a position to recover from the ravages of this. The only document that is available that is available, that of the King List, only cites that "Awan was touched with weapons" and, following the incident (whatever it was) the kingship returned to Kish. Kish.

A variety of dynasties followed, including The Second Dynasty of Kish, the kingdom of Hamazi along with Hamazi's Dynasty of Erech however, there isn't any historical proof of the timeframes of any of these. It is impossible to know the exact events that occurred, however having the reigning monarchy of Hamazi is an obvious sign that Sumer was struggling to restore its power.

After that, came the King, who was able to brought back Sumer to its former glory. The name of the king was Lugalannemundu and as per the King List reigned for the time of ninety years. He was a formidable leader in the military and a strategist who was able to take over vast areas, according to a report that was found, and a copy was found. The original was lost and could or might not turn to light at some time.

The document describes King Lugalannemundu is called "king over the entire universe." Lugalannemundu was capable of have all nations of the world give him a homage and then brought peace. It was he who brought Sumer to its previous splendor.

The same document also is a description of a revolt planned by the ruling officials (ensi's) of the thirteen city-states. They were determined to take down the king but he was able to squelch their revolt.

Based on the data we have received we can conclude that Lugalannemendu was an imposing King, whose influence was felt across many regions. For the duration during his rule, it is likely ruled during the year 262 BC.

About 2500 BC A King named Mesilim was crowned Kish's ruler. Kish. The influence of Mesilim was enormous and he was able to rule over a vast area and played a significant part in the border dispute that arose with Umma as well as Lagash. He was succeeded by Ur-

Nanshe who created the dynasty that continued to rule for the following five generations. It is not clear how he got to the top and what his motivations were, but judging from the number of documents were left behind by him it is clear that his reign was one of victory.

One phrase is found in several of the inscriptions that have been discovered: "The Ships of Dilmun provided him with wood as a homage from other countries." This suggests that his influence and influence was far-reaching beyond Sumer. But, aside from the frequently repeated assertion There is no additional evidence to back this claim.

Ur-Nanshe's grandson Eannatum was a key person in Sumerian time. In a short period of time, he was crowned with the title of King of Kish that was associated with supremacy over the entire Sumer. The first years of his rule were marked by the efforts to restore damaged parts within the nation. Then, it was the time that he began to undertake military campaigns which earned his power and along with it, an indefatigable spot into the history of Sumerian civilization.

The motives behind his military actions is unanswered. His victory over Umma towards the north however, was outlined in a document written by one of archivists for the King. The document also assists in unravel the earlier-mentioned conflict about the borders between cities like Umma as well as Lagash.

In the time of Mesilim the two cities got into an argument about their borders. In a state of insolvency, unable to resolve the issue independently the two cities pleaded with Mesilim who they explicitly acknowledged as their ruler, to help them find the best solution. The king consulted Sataran, god of conflict, for guidance, and following a visit to his oracle, offered a resolution which both cities agreed to.

It is a typical instance where one party received a shorter end of the stick in this case that was Umma. Umma. The city was not long until the ensi of the city broke their promise that they made Mesilim and the leader of Lagash. Their army crossed the border in accordance with the agreement and took over a portion of the northern region of Lagash.

The situation was unchanged until Eannatum was able to rectify the mistake and led his troops to Enakalle and ensi of Umma. The ensi was defeated by the Ummaites and signed an accord with them to reestablish the border again. He also turned a section of the area near the border of Umma into a no-man's area, in order to reduce the chance of a possible conflict.

Eannatum also established his authority by removing the forces of King Zuzu who was his ruler from Akshak who attempted to conduct to attack Kish, the capital city. Kish. Eannatum led an army that was able to repel the attack and fought off the invaders and inflicted heavy losses on the attackers. Following this victory, he was awarded the name "King of Kish."

A couple of years of peace followed and he took advantage of this peace to begin building a new canal in Lagash. Lagash. But, before the construction was finished, he was forced to fight his enemies again. Elamites swarmed out of the west, and threatened his rule. He was able to take down the army of the Elamites and return them to their homes however, he didn't have the resources needed to mount a counter-attack and conquer Elam.

Another threat was in the direction of northern Europe, and included army units from Kish as well as Akshak. He managed to construct an effective defense, however immediately afterward, Elamites returned. The famous king was successful in repelling the subsequent attacks, and ultimately establishing peace for the second time.

However, his reign came to an abrupt end. It is not clear the cause of his death however it is likely that he died in a fight. Following his death his brother, who was known as Enannatum was crowned the king. He was in a privileged situation when Umma's city Umma was restored to its full power and was a major threat to his rule. However, after strengthening the boundaries of Lagash and assembling the forces and launched an offensive against the enemies of Lagash.

He was able to meet his forces from Umma along with their allies for an epic battle. The forces of Lagash were headed by Enannatum's son Entemen. In the field of battle the army of Lagash delivered a decisive blow against the Ummaites winning a full victory and leading their leader, Ur-Lumma to a furious retreat.

It turned out that they wouldn't have much chance to celebrate the victory because a new foe was soon to emerge. The man known as Il the Head of the temple of The city of Hallab. When the war among Umma as well as Lagash was completed, he launched an assault on the weaker armies of Entemena in the region of Lagash. While he was unable to take Lagash it self, he established himself as the leader of Umma and, just as that, the previous rivalry between the two cities came back.

While it was a difficult circumstance, it appears that the issue was not settled in war , but rather through an agreement. This was probably forced on them by another third party - the ruler from another country who had the power over the entire Sumer and other areas.

There were other kings who were followed, whose actions weren't as well-documented and, according to all accounts, didn't attain the same success than their predecessors. The king Urukagina then came to the throne. He was acclaimed for his comprehensive reformative Act which was discussed in depth in Chapter 3 within the "Law" subheading.

Urukagina's regime, though significant however, it was not a lengthy one. The man who ended his rule was the man dubbed Lugalzaggesi. As the ruler of close-by Umma, Lugalzaggesi looted and destroyed the city of Lagash and set fire to everything including temples. But, based on the unearthed documents, it is clear that his rule ended the same way as it began. His death was from the fate of Sargon the Great after around two years of rule.

Sargon who was dubbed "the great" by historians of the past is a different truly amazing character in the time of the Near East. Sargon's influence wasn't limited to Sumer only, but expanded into India as well as Egypt. His military and political activities are well-documented.

While being from Semitic Origin, Sargon started as a high official serving Ur-Zbaba who was a King of Kish. It is possible the case that Ur-Zbaba had his throne removed and executed during the same time period which resulted with the demise of Lagash and the dethronement of Urukagina, the king.

So, when he rose to the limelight, Sargon made it his first priority in order to drag Lugalzagessi to the ground. Sargon launched an unexpected attack at his capital city, Erech, ruining its walls and scattering its guards. Despite Erech's allies arriving to aid and Lugalzagessi's return with his army, since they were on a mission but they proved in no way a threat to Sargon The Great. Lugalzagessi was dragged in chains to Nippur, the city. Nippur.

His war continued with his assault on Ur. of Ur. After defeating Ur to the brink of collapse, Sargon began to take on Umma and complete his conquer of the entirety of Sumer. From then on Sargon turned his attention to other areas and extended his rule more. In the final days of his reign in the year 1898, he was able to command a huge area and an impressive amount of soldiers.

Rimush succeeded to his grandfather Sargon as a king. Rimush was confronted with the challenges that the later large empires had to deal with, including numerous internal revolts and revolts. Both him and his brother Manishtushu who ascended to the throne just nine years after, had to battle numerous battles to ensure their empire was afloat. Manishtushu however, walked following the steps of his father and set out to conquer new territories.

Manishtushu became the successor of his son, Naram-Sin. At first, he also won a number of impressive military victories, thereby advancing his firmament and expanding the territory. But, as it usually happens the great dynasty finally ended. Barbaric Hordes made up of Gutains coming from east invaded and threatened to bring a waist on cities like Agade which was the capital of the empire.

According to a mythological version of the events, Naram-Sin's death was caused by the fact that Naram-Sin destroyed Nippur's city Nippur and committed a sin against the god of supreme Enlil. Enlil was the god who created the Gutains on Agade to take revenge for this abominable act.

If we choose to take this standard Sumerian argument or not. The truth is that Gutians originated to the hills and then turned Agade into dust. Once a beautiful city was entirely and totally devastated by the barbarian tribes that had no respect about their Sumerian culture or civilisation.

In the wake of this defeat and the demise of Naram-Sin Sumer fell into confusion and chaos. Naram-Sin's son managed to restore just a little of the glory his family enjoyed. He claimed a few successes of his own however these were not fights to grow or to conquer, but rather to live. Sharkalisharri was the son of Naram-Sin was forced to settle in his city Agade and its immediate environs.

The Gutians who took over the entire political power following Naram-Sin's demise, turned Lagash into their capital. They have, perhaps surprisingly have adopted many of Urukagina's ideas reforms, hoping to please God and gain their approval.

A number of Gutian rulers reigned over Sumer in the 8 or 9 centuries following victory over Naram Sin. Similar to the previous Sumerian rulers, the Gutian Ensi's debated and battled among themselves, attempting to establish absolute power and independence of their city-states.

The closing of Sumerian culture as we are familiar with it took place during the reign of Rim Sin. In his time in the 1750s BC when the once-insignificant city of Babylon became a major player. It was ruled by Hammurabi, the Semitic Hammurabi, the ruler of Semitic Hammurabi, Babylonians launched an assault against Rim-Sin as well as other notable leaders of the time. The campaign was successful and he was made the supreme ruler of the vast region stretching from to the Habur River to the Persian Gulf.

This year marks the turning point for Sumerian time period. This is when Sumer is over and a new one, Babylonia, built on its foundations, starts.

Chapter 10: Secret Life Of Sumer

Each chapter will have provided you with an overall picture about the Sumerian state, starting from fundamental geographical details to their morals, religion and beliefs, to significant events and individuals who played an important role in their growth. This chapter will examine some of the lesser-known details and theories regarding Sumer and its history.

As we've already observed many of the things we are aware of (or think we have learned) about the ancient civilization is shrouded by a veil of mystery. The historic resources that we have are usually a mix of both imagination and fact And a lot of "facts" are founded on myths or broad interpretations of the Scribes.

A mystery which captivates the attention of modern researchers of today is the meaning of Annunakis smaller gods who are believed to have been children of the original god, An.

There's an entire school of thought that supports the notion that Annunaki were in reality powerful aliens who protected the human race from the devastating floods and then provided them with various tools and techniques required to sustain and develop the civilization.

The amount of truth with this idea is anyone's guess. There are certain aspects of the Sumerian mythology that would appear to be in support of it at least as much as the notion of a bunch of gods deciding the future of human civilization. Of of course, a larger portion of the academic community is against this idea as ridiculous.

Moving back to more concrete issues, Sumerians were the first to establish libraries as that we see it in the present. They threw away all the important documents and writings in their schools , and developed an efficient method of preserving older tablets by writing and recounting.

It was also their first civilization that made a practical utilization of wheels. It's not clear which civilization was the first to create it, but we can say with a reasonable amount of conviction that Sumerians were the first to put its potential to use. The earliest references to the wheel can be found in different places than Mesopotamia which means it's probable that the Sumerians were the first to learn about the concept, and then figured out how to get the most of it.

It is also possible that the concept of credit originated in old Sumer. As we've already seen the role of the concept of prosperity and wealth played an important aspect for the Sumerians and it's easy to imagine that the more prosperous people in society provided their clients the option to purchase items and services in multiple increments. Based on the few evidences that we have today the laws that governed this type of commerce were very rigorous and protected both sides from possible exploitation.

Written contracts are also a result of Sumer. This isn't really remarkable, given the fact that Sumerians were the ones who came up with the first written contracts, however it's still remarkable that they had the foresight to realize in the early days that the most effective method of protecting the interests of their clients was to have everything in writing, in order that later disputes could be settled easily.

Conclusion

Sumerian mythology remains a mystery for many thousands of years. In fact, up to in the 19th century and 18th century there was little to know regarding the goddesses and gods from the Sumerian pantheon. Also, little was made of the people who fought them. The stories of the world's first real civilization are now being brought to the public captivating both women and men across the globe. The tales that tell the tales of Enkidu, Nanna, Enlil, Ereshkigal, and Gilgamesh are reaching new audiences, including men and women who want to know more about a different culture from our one we live in. Sumerian mythology is so influential that their gods were able to be incorporated into other societies, the most famous example being Aphrodite who was born as Inanna. When you read Sumerian Mythology: A fascinating Sumerian History and Mesopotamian Empire and Myths, you learnt the stories of gods and the great men. These are the stories that comprise an epic canon in Sumerian religion.

Sumerian civilization has secretly been an important part of the way we are living today. We are largely unaware of the fact that it has occurred. The way we gauge time, study the sky as well as the way we cultivate and plant crops has a lot in have to do with the innovations that were made by the Sumerians over six millennia back. Additionally, it was heroes such as Gilgamesh who defined what is an individual hero in the modern world. They were heroes who were gods, earning their spot on the throne in a variety of ways. The Sumerians relied on their stories to provide guidelines for other people on the way to live their lives and to to understand their position within the larger world. Sumerian Mythology: Fascinating Sumerian History and Mesopotamian Myths and Empire gave you the earliest stories of heroes and gods to assist you in understanding the who and what are the Sumerians were and why they were so important.

Sumerian Mythology: Fascinating Sumerian History and Mesopotamian Empire and Myths examined the stories of heroes and gods. These myths of heroes and gods were incredibly important to Mesopotamian people. Studying about these myths is the way to come to comprehend the life they experienced and how it differed from the one we live in today. It was a land of birds, with appearance of giants and gods who had wings like birds, and beautiful goddesses who symbolized marriage to the kings of various cities-states. The Sumerians shared a variety of stories about gods such as Utu, Nanna, An, Ashur, and Inanna tales which made the empires of Mesopotamia last for more than 4000 years. In actual fact, European travelers to the Near East in the 18th century realized that there were still areas in which Goddess Inanna (more than 5000 years old at the time) was revered in the shadows.

The culture of the Sumerians was quite different from ours. The people who were at the center of Sumerian civilization - who lived in the present-day Iraq, Kuwait, Syria and other areas These people comprised a society that was so different from the way we see and think about our world today that it is nearly impossible to recognize. Sumerian Mythology: Fascinating Sumerian history and Mesopotamian Myths and Empires offered you a lens to view the world of their people. It was a land of great empires, including those of the Akkadian, Hurrian, Assyrian and Babylonian. It was a place with a legend of beauty and wealth.

Your journey began by studying the Sumerians by studying their culture. Sumer was regarded as the oldest civilization known to mankind that reached dizzy heights in excess of a thousand years prior to Egypt. They constructed ziggurats which touched the sky, and gardens that flooded in the channels that fed their agricultural fields. It was in many aspects that Sumer seemed like a dream. If their gods were any guide there was never easy sailing. The chapter in this section you will learn that Sumer went through several difficult times of unification, with the beginning in an Akkadian Empire. In this period, an extensive process towards Akkadian becoming the replacement for Sumerian as the primary local language started.

Sumerian society was extremely complex as any society that is typical of the major civilizations. At the heart of the society was the city-state. on top of the city-state were the priests and the kings. Both groups were engaged in an intricate dance, however it was a significant one. Similar to Egypt the rulers of Sumer were aware that a secure rule required them to recognize and promote religion in concrete ways. This is perhaps the reason why the Sumerian rulers wrote numerous tablets in which they boasted about the construction of the temple of this or that and being in favour of the god of this goddess or that. The King were of Sumerian city-states and the rulers who followed them later in the empires, also were married to goddesses in symbolic ways, like Inanna. If this doesn't provide you with an understanding of the significance religious beliefs played within their culture it is unlikely that anything else can.

www.ingramcontent.com/pod-product-compliance
Lightning Source LLC
Chambersburg PA
CBHW050025130526
44590CB00042B/1908